What Life Was Like®

AMONG SAMURAI AND SHOGUNS

Japan
AD 1000 ~ 1700

What Life Was Like

AMONG SAMURAI AND SHOGUNS

Japan
AD 1000 - 1700

BY THE EDITORS OF TIME-LIFE BOOKS, ALEXANDRIA, VIRGINIA

CONTENTS

Among Samurai
and Shoguns

IN THE LAND OF THE RISING SUN

"Go! and may prosperity attend thy dynasty, and may it, like Heaven and Earth, endure for ever." With this command, the sun goddess Amaterasu sent her grandson Ninigi to rule over Japan. Ninigi descended from the heavens to the southern Japanese island of Kyushu, but there he remained, leaving it to his great-grandson Jimmu to fulfill Amaterasu's wish. Jimmu journeyed to the main island of Honshu, where he became the first emperor of the Land of the Rising Sun.

This tale of Japan's beginning is related in the *Nihon Shoki,* or *Chronicles of Japan.* By the early 700s, when the story was set down, Japan's many clans had placed themselves under the reign of an imperial family who claimed to trace its origins to Jimmu. This dynasty founded a long-lasting capital in Nara, drawing inspiration for its de-

sign from China. Earlier, the Japanese court had used a Chinese model for a series of political reforms known as the Taika, aimed at strengthening the central government.

Indeed, Japan benefited from a steady flow of Chinese thought and technology in the areas of medicine, literature, art, mathematics, and agriculture brought by Chinese and Korean immigrants. From Korean traders, the Japanese also acquired a new religion, Buddhism, which had made its way from India to China and then to Korea. According to the *Nihon Shoki,* a sixth-century Korean ruler had sent the Japanese court a Buddhist image and scriptures and a personal message: "This doctrine is amongst all doctrines the most excellent."

The Japanese did not adopt the Chinese way of life unswervingly, however. In the Japanese court, for example, there would be no periodic changes of dynasty because of a loss of heavenly mandate, as there were in China. Each Japanese emperor was chosen only from the original imperial family, who were considered the divine

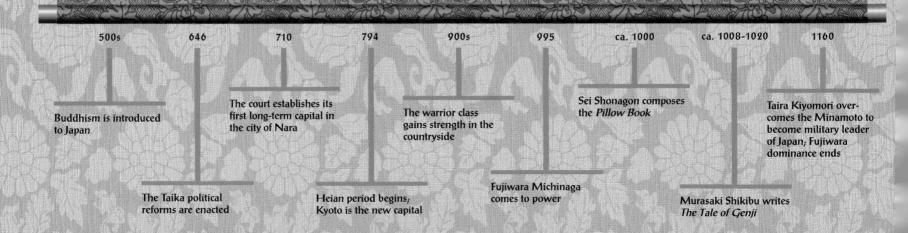

| 500s | 646 | 710 | 794 | 900s | 995 | ca. 1000 | ca. 1008-1020 | 1160 |

Buddhism is introduced to Japan

The Taika political reforms are enacted

The court establishes its first long-term capital in the city of Nara

Heian period begins; Kyoto is the new capital

The warrior class gains strength in the countryside

Fujiwara Michinaga comes to power

Sei Shonagon composes the *Pillow Book*

Murasaki Shikibu writes *The Tale of Genji*

Taira Kiyomori overcomes the Minamoto to become military leader of Japan; Fujiwara dominance ends

descendants of the sun goddess. But Japanese emperors, especially after the Nara period, were usually political figureheads. A member of another powerful family controlled important matters of state.

During the Heian period, which began in 794 and was marked by the move of the capital to Kyoto, that powerful family was the Fujiwara, who acted as regents to the emperors. Fujiwara Michinaga, who assumed power in 995, was the greatest of the Heian regents.

One of Michinaga's ancestors, the first Fujiwara regent, wrote, "There is a sacred and ancient saying that Japan is a land blessed by the muses." The literature of the Heian era gave proof to his words. Much of the poetry and prose of this time was written in Chinese, for the Japanese had adopted China's writing system centuries before. A person writing in Japanese used a modified, syllabic system known as kana. Women, most of them not schooled in Chinese, wrote in that script. Two acclaimed masterpieces by women in this period are Sei

Shonagon's *Pillow Book,* with its trenchant observations of court life, and Murasaki Shikibu's *Tale of Genji,* detailing the romances and intrigues of the Heian court.

Outside Kyoto, in the countryside, people fought to protect their lands from interlopers. The warrior class—including the aristocratic fighters called samurai—grew stronger as the Heian period wore on. Japan's urban aristocracy lost control of the government at the end of the 12th century, when two powerful military clans, the Taira and the Minamoto, battled for supremacy. Finally, in the city of Kamakura, Minamoto leader Yoritomo established a military government known as the Kamakura *bakufu* and in 1192 became shogun of Japan.

The samurai of Japan were an impressive sight in their lacquered iron armor, armed with sword, dagger, and bow. They pledged loyalty to their daimyo, or local lords, and to the shogun and willingly fought for honor, glory, and booty. But the peaceful first decades of the bakufu offered little opportunity for battle and advance-

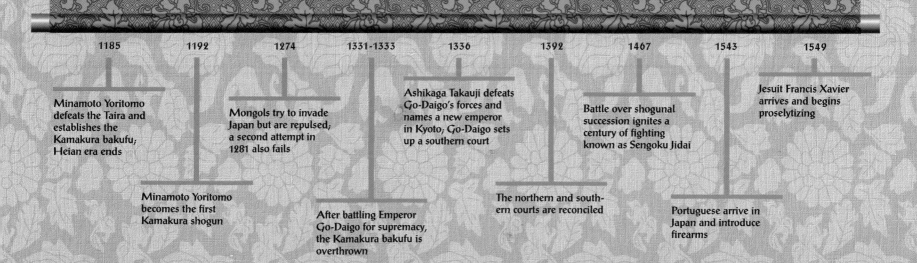

1185 Minamoto Yoritomo defeats the Taira and establishes the Kamakura bakufu; Heian era ends

1192 Minamoto Yoritomo becomes the first Kamakura shogun

1274 Mongols try to invade Japan but are repulsed; a second attempt in 1281 also fails

1331-1333 After battling Emperor Go-Daigo for supremacy, the Kamakura bakufu is overthrown

1336 Ashikaga Takauji defeats Go-Daigo's forces and names a new emperor in Kyoto; Go-Daigo sets up a southern court

1392 The northern and southern courts are reconciled

1467 Battle over shogunal succession ignites a century of fighting known as Sengoku Jidai

1543 Portuguese arrive in Japan and introduce firearms

1549 Jesuit Francis Xavier arrives and begins proselytizing

ment. That changed in 1274 when Khubilai Khan launched an invasion of Japan. Samurai rose to the challenge, racing to Hakata Bay, off Kyushu, to meet the Mongol ships. With the help of typhoon winds, the Japanese repulsed the invaders.

A shortage of land to reward its vassals for such service threatened the bakufu's stability. And in the 1330s, Emperor Go-Daigo's forces took over. But Go-Daigo was later forced to flee Kyoto when he was defeated by warlord Ashikaga Takauji at Minato River. While Go-Daigo set up a court in the south, Takauji placed a second emperor on Kyoto's throne. Civil war raged until 1392, when the southern emperor agreed to step down.

In 1467 a battle over shogunal succession led to a century of warfare—a situation that proved beneficial to the economy. Merchants thrived as the daimyo's need for weapons, armor, and basic necessities rose, and guilds and other organizations formed to safely transport goods.

Art flourished as well. Architecture, sculpture, and ceramics blossomed, and metalworking became an art in itself. Great war romances, historical works, and poetry proliferated. One of the greatest artistic achievements was No theater, a stylized form of drama born of a synthesis of poetry, dance, and music.

During this same period, Buddhism became more widespread; Zen Buddhism, with its emphasis on self-reliance, had a particular appeal to the samurai. The 16th century saw the arrival of another religion—Christianity—brought by the Jesuit missionaries following in the wake of Portuguese traders.

The traders had introduced their own novelty: firearms. Among those exploiting the new weapons was the warlord Oda Nobunaga, who seized Kyoto in 1568 and took the first steps toward unifying Japan. When Nobunaga fell to an assassin, Toyotomi Hideyoshi seized power; he became overlord of all 66 Japanese provinces.

Seeking new land and avenues of trade, Hideyoshi sent forces into Korea in the 1590s, a venture doomed to

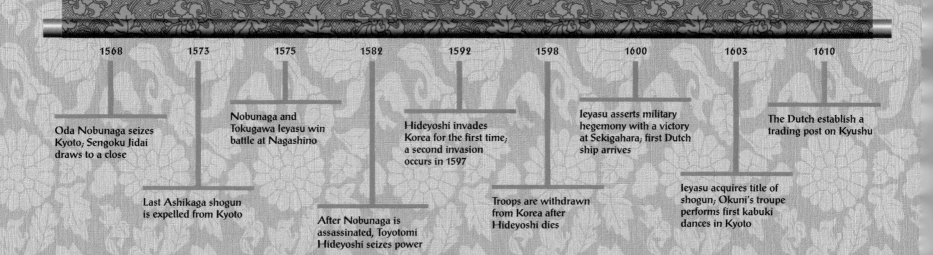

1568 Oda Nobunaga seizes Kyoto; Sengoku Jidai draws to a close

1573 Last Ashikaga shogun is expelled from Kyoto

1575 Nobunaga and Tokugawa Ieyasu win battle at Nagashino

1582 After Nobunaga is assassinated, Toyotomi Hideyoshi seizes power

1592 Hideyoshi invades Korea for the first time; a second invasion occurs in 1597

1598 Troops are withdrawn from Korea after Hideyoshi dies

1600 Ieyasu asserts military hegemony with a victory at Sekigahara; first Dutch ship arrives

1603 Ieyasu acquires title of shogun; Okuni's troupe performs first kabuki dances in Kyoto

1610 The Dutch establish a trading post on Kyushu

failure. Hideyoshi died in 1598, and from the ensuing struggle for control emerged the man who would realize the goal of a lasting peace: Tokugawa Ieyasu. He established the Tokugawa shogunate in 1603, and 12 years later vanquished his last rival by besieging Osaka Castle and forcing its master, Hideyoshi's son, to commit suicide.

To maintain peace and stability, the Tokugawa developed a structured society, one that did not include proselytizing Christians. Ieyasu had welcomed the Dutch in 1600 in large part because they offered trade without trying to convert the Japanese. By the mid-1610s, Ieyasu expelled the missionaries, and two decades later, Japan closed its borders to all but a handful of foreign traders.

Japan prospered under Tokugawa peace. Merchants thrived, and in the late 1600s, their wealth fueled a vibrant new era, the Genroku. Kabuki and puppet theater, popular literature, and art flourished, and the pleasure quarters of the major cities never slept. The colorful and exciting lifestyle of the period was given the name "the floating world," and it proved to be fleeting as well. Amid a series of devastating natural disasters, the Genroku period came to an end in 1704.

The Tokugawa shogunate continued for another century and a half, but its authority deteriorated. During this time, Japan continued its policy of seclusion, turning away European trading ships. Then in 1853 American commodore Matthew Perry appeared in Edo Bay with a squadron of warships. Perry claimed to seek only trade and good treatment for any American seaman who might need aid. But the threat to Japan was implicit. When Perry returned the next year, with a bigger force, a treaty for limited trade was negotiated. Treaties with other countries followed. In 1868 opponents of the Tokugawa regime overthrew the shogunate and restored governing power to the emperor and his ruling clique. And just as it had once adapted Chinese ideas, Japan began importing Western concepts, methods, and institutions and fitting them to its own unique culture.

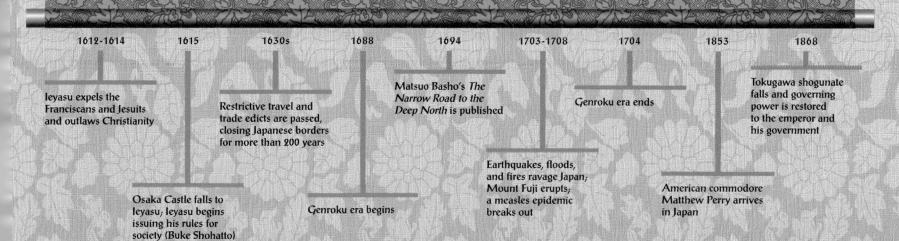

| 1612–1614 | 1615 | 1630s | 1688 | 1694 | 1703–1708 | 1704 | 1853 | 1868 |

Ieyasu expels the Franciscans and Jesuits and outlaws Christianity

Osaka Castle falls to Ieyasu; Ieyasu begins issuing his rules for society (Buke Shohatto)

Restrictive travel and trade edicts are passed, closing Japanese borders for more than 200 years

Genroku era begins

Matsuo Basho's *The Narrow Road to the Deep North* is published

Earthquakes, floods, and fires ravage Japan; Mount Fuji erupts; a measles epidemic breaks out

Genroku era ends

American commodore Matthew Perry arrives in Japan

Tokugawa shogunate falls and governing power is restored to the emperor and his government

Japan is an island nation composed of four principal land-masses: Honshu, Kyushu, Shikoku, and Hokkaido, though Hokkaido was not claimed by the Japanese until the latter part of the 19th century. Its nearest neighbors on the mainland are Korea and China, the former lying 120 miles from the western coast of Kyushu, the latter 500 miles. For most of its early history, Japan's isolated location protected it from foreign aggression, except in the late 13th century when Khubilai Khan attempted to land forces on Kyushu, at Hakata Bay. The Japanese leader Toyotomi Hideyoshi returned the favor three centuries later, invading Korea and capturing Seoul before being turned back.

Primarily mountainous and heavily forested, Japan has only a limited amount of arable land. Chief among the tracts suitable for farming are Kanto plain, site of Edo (Tokyo), city of the Tokugawa shoguns; Nobi plain, home to Nagoya, birthplace of the 16th-century warlord Oda Nobunaga; and Kinai plain, where the eighth-century capital of Nara and the Heian imperial city of Kyoto lie. Throughout its history, the island kingdom's 17,000-mile-long coastline has provided it with plenty of seafood to supplement the agricultural staple, rice.

Japan's rugged mountain peaks, blossoming cherry trees, terraced hillsides, rushing streams, and deep seas have inspired its people throughout the centuries. Not everyone could afford a screen painted with exquisite scenes of nature, but even a poor man traveling the Tokai-do highway from Edo to Kyoto could look up to see glorious Mount Fuji. The 17th-century poet Basho was not a rich man, but he was an avid traveler who knew that just around the bend another breathtaking view awaited: "I wandered all by myself into the heart of the mountains of Yoshino. White masses of clouds were piled up over the peaks, and all the valleys were filled with smoky rain."

MONGOLIA

•Beijing

CHINA

YELLOW SEA

MANCHURIA

HOKKAIDO

SEA OF JAPAN

HONSHU

Seoul

KOREA

OKI ISLANDS

J A P A N

Tokaido • Edo (Tokyo)

Lake Biwa • Sekigahara Mt. Fuji ▲ • Kamakura

Kyoto Hakone

Yodo River • Nagoya

Hyogo • Osaka • Ueno

TSUSHIMA Nara • Ise

INLAND SEA

IKI SHIKOKU

Hakata

BEPPU BAY PACIFIC OCEAN

Nagasaki

KYUSHU

EAST CHINA SEA

TANEGASHIMA

N

CHAPTER ONE

The Court of the Shining Prince

These aristocrats of Japan's Heian period (AD 794-1185) could be setting off to participate in the imperial moon-viewing festival. During this celebration, members of the court spent the night floating on lakes in the palace gardens, gazing at the full moon and composing poems. Festivals, religious celebrations, and political intrigue ruled the lives of the court.

 A lone figure stood in the garden of Kyoto's Hojoji Buddhist Temple, contemplating its new Golden Hall as the rising sun bathed the shining green roof tiles, golden door, and lustrous white walls in a cheerful radiance. Fujiwara Michinaga had barely slept. All night long, he had searched his mind for any task left undone in preparing for this long-awaited August morning in AD 1022. Today the hall would be dedicated, and Michinaga, head of the powerful Fujiwara clan, was determined that the spectacle would rival imperial enthronements and weddings.

Over the past few days, people had been flocking to the city of Kyoto. Ox-drawn carriages had clogged the capital's streets. Anticipating the arrival of so many conveyances, Michinaga had created a vast open space by breaking down the earthen wall of the temple complex on the east. Now the site was crammed with vehicles resting on huge spoked wheels. There were the large Chinese-style carriages, high off the ground, splendidly lacquered and decorated, fitted out with silk curtains and opulent furnishings, each topped with a green gabled roof. Only the imperial family and officials of the highest rank were permitted to own them. Thatched roofs graced the vehicles of second-, third-, and fourth-rank aristocrats, while men and women of lesser status had to content themselves with a simple structure of poles with wooden boards for a floor and a roof of stretched straw. The owners of these conveyances had squeezed into them as many as four passengers, who sat on simple straw mats.

East of the temple complex, the Kamo River had also been crowded for days, brimming with rafts bearing gifts from provincial governors. When the vessels were unloaded, it looked as if, a writer noted, "treasures must have rained down from Heaven, and the four directions given up their stores." This too was a process set in motion by Michinaga. He had ordered the gift giving and was gratified to see that a competition among the provincial governors had resulted in offerings outstanding in number and magnificence.

There were some activities, however, that even Michinaga could not control. At the gates of

ing empress, Ishi, had arrived with their ladies-in-waiting the night before the dedication and had been accommodated in sleeping quarters within the temple complex. For this event, each noblewoman selected the colors of her robes and the particular leaf, flower, or sea motifs that made up the patterns. The result was a kaleidoscope of silks, in exquisite shades of red, green, blue, yellow, reddish purple, and pink.

The women wore red damask trousers, stiffened by an added layer of cloth placed between the lining and the outer shell. Over these, they donned several robes of shiny peeled silk, in subtly harmonizing colors. The fabric was made by stretching the silk on a

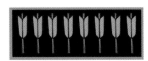

waxed, lacquered board, spread with paste. After the paste dried, the cloth was peeled off, displaying a glossy sheen. The top items of apparel, more highly decorated and of heavier silk than the oth-

"Poetry seemed to be having bad karma that day."

the temple complex, a throng of common people pressed forward for a glimpse of the ongoing events. Many were poor mountain folk who had worked for days, dyeing, patching, and stitching together whatever fabric they owned to create their own finery. A special detachment of police wearing red hunting robes tried to contain them. At the public dance rehearsal held a few days prior to the dedication, Michinaga had viewed the crowding commoners with disdain. "They aren't an attractive sight," he observed. He insisted that they be restrained, but as soon as the police beat these spectators back, they thrust forward again. The crowd was especially eager to catch sight of the ladies of the court in all their splendor.

The two grand empresses, Shoshi and Kenshi, and the reign-

ers, were a jacket and a skirt with a train up to three yards long.

The robes were made so that each sleeve was shorter than the one below it, producing a cascade of layered colors at the wrists, a tantalizing sight as they hung over the sides of carriages or were glimpsed through the slats of window blinds. On the day of the dedication, sightseers gaped with delight at such attractive, if fleeting, visions. As one writer exclaimed, "How splendid it was to think that the adornments of heavenly beings must certainly be similar."

But the best was yet to come. The crowd milling outside the compound's gates could hear the gentle notes echoing from two music boats floating on the complex's garden lake, where players were delicately plucking six-, seven-, and 13-string kotos, striking

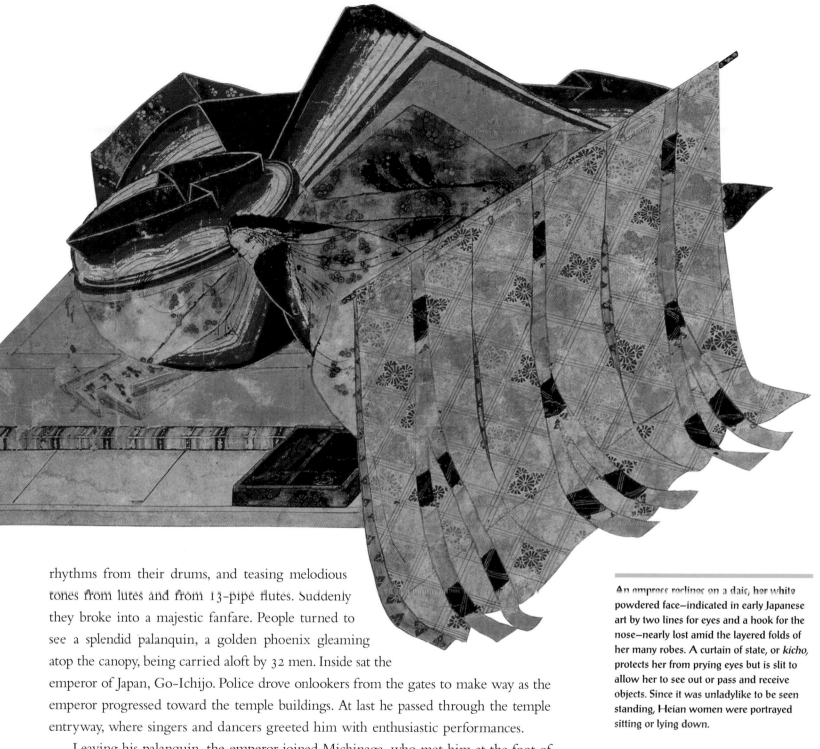

rhythms from their drums, and teasing melodious tones from lutes and from 13-pipe flutes. Suddenly they broke into a majestic fanfare. People turned to see a splendid palanquin, a golden phoenix gleaming atop the canopy, being carried aloft by 32 men. Inside sat the emperor of Japan, Go-Ichijo. Police drove onlookers from the gates to make way as the emperor progressed toward the temple buildings. At last he passed through the temple entryway, where singers and dancers greeted him with enthusiastic performances.

Leaving his palanquin, the emperor joined Michinaga, who met him at the foot of a flight of stairs and proceeded to escort him to a large statue of the Buddha. There, as custom dictated, the emperor of Japan bowed before the sacred image. Watching this age-old tradition, Michinaga could not restrain his tears. Soon the crown prince joined

An empress reclines on a dais, her white powdered face—indicated in early Japanese art by two lines for eyes and a hook for the nose—nearly lost amid the layered folds of her many robes. A curtain of state, or *kicho,* protects her from prying eyes but is slit to allow her to see out or pass and receive objects. Since it was unladylike to be seen standing, Heian women were portrayed sitting or lying down.

the assemblage, and the celebrations were under way.

Around noon, to the tinkle of bells, guests were served a meal, the imperial ladies receiving theirs in beautifully crafted boxes of cypress wood. The food probably consisted of rice cakes, pickled fish, seaweed, several kinds of vegetables—including carrots, onions, radishes, and eggplant—and nuts, with perhaps pomegranates and oranges offered as delicacies. Most diners washed down their food with rice wine.

For the elite, it was a grand day of eating, listening to music, responding appropriately to the reading of sacred texts, and watching lion, butterfly, and bird dances. The scents of sandalwood and many blossoms filled the compound, rising from silver and gold censers. Finally, red-lacquered chests filled with gifts were distributed. Michinaga's dedication had been a triumph, "a marvel of marvels," as one observer put it, "never to be duplicated."

The emperor, revered as the descendant of the Shinto sun goddess, had performed his ceremonial duties and received the deference due him, but the main focus of attention was the all-powerful Fujiwara Michinaga. Although he himself currently held no office, his influence outweighed such formalities. Most of the nobles owed their offices to him, including the emperor and the crown prince (both of them were grandsons of Michinaga), all three empresses (his daughters), and the regent (his son).

Michinaga's clan, the Fujiwara, had been the dominant power in Japan since the eighth century AD and would retain its strength until the late 12th century, a period known as the Heian, or Peace and Tranquillity, era. The Fujiwara directed all governmental policies, wielding full sovereign power. They also monopolized court offices through political shrewdness. But they did not achieve their right to rule by commanding armies or by the birth of sons into a monarchy. Rather their power rested on two important factors: the wealth gained from the control of rice fields and the marriages of their daughters.

Heian aristocrats sought to include beauty and poetry in every aspect of their lives, even on military saddles *(above)* and cosmetic boxes *(right)*. To please their patrons, artisans decorated their work with poetic imagery and developed new techniques to enhance it artistically, such as adding gold dust to lacquer.

Mother-of-pearl and branches of clover embellish the black lacquer of the saddle here. On the box, the design of cartwheels seasoning in water, a popular Heian theme, is made of gold dust, mother-of-pearl, and precious metal foil.

Rice was Japan's most important commodity. During the seventh century, political changes had made all rice land the property of the emperor. Farmers were granted rights to cultivate the land but were heavily taxed for the privilege. With this system in place, the emperor could maintain power over the country. But from the beginning, certain land was protected from taxation. The emperor allotted rights to wholly or partially tax-exempt plots to court nobles, the Fujiwara among them, and religious institutions. As the centuries progressed, many aristocratic families gathered more land. By the 10th century, Michinaga's family held more rice fields, and hence more power, than any other family.

Rice wealth gave the Fujiwara influence in court, but their daughters' marriages took them to the pinnacle of power—the regency of Japan—and helped them maintain it for centuries. It was a remarkable hereditary system in which female offspring were extremely important; what the Fujiwara inherited was the right to marry their daughters into the royal family and thereby to serve as regents for their docile imperial grandsons. Each emperor understood that he might become an ex-emperor at the will of the regent and usually did as instructed by the leader of the Fujiwara family's most influential faction.

During the regency of Michinaga, the most outstanding leader the Fujiwara clan had ever known, the Heian age reached its apex. Opulence characterized the period, and the immense wealth that accrued to the nobles was displayed with exquisite taste. To the aristocracy, it was artistic sensitivity as much as wealth and position that determined an individual's worth. Heian-era nobles judged one another's ingenuity in creating poetry, music, and painting; cleverness in playing games and making conversation; grace in movement; and the elegance of certain possessions, especially clothing. In this society, two women rose to lasting prominence because of their literary talents: Murasaki Shikibu, author of the acclaimed novel *The Tale of Genji*, and Sei Shonagon, an outstanding diarist. In her *Pillow Book*, Sei commented with extraordinary wit and insight on the manners and activities of her contemporaries.

For the aristocrats of the Heian world, life centered around beautiful Kyoto. They disdained the outlying provinces. But as the centuries passed, power would slowly shift from the city elite to the countryside, where overlords and warriors known as samurai developed their bases of power, and all that Fujiwara Michinaga had built would be threatened.

Michinaga's father, Kaneie, had followed the pattern set by previous Fujiwara leaders by marrying his eldest daughter to the emperor and his second daughter to the crown prince, who later became emperor. Kaneie subsequently moved into the powerful position of regent when the throne came to his six-year-old grandson Ichijo. As soon as possible, Kaneie appointed his sons and close relations to high office. To pass on his acquired power, Kaneie resigned the regency, shortly before he died in 990, in favor of his eldest son.

Michinaga was not the eldest, but rather the third of Kaneie's trio of favored sons. A contemporary characterized him as "tactful, manly and pious." He had good judgment, kept his temper in check, looked after the interests of friends and followers, and showed sensitivity to the feelings of others. It was said that in his youth he had "avoided casual flirtations—not from any absurdly rigid scruples, but simply because he was unwilling to make an enemy or cause a woman pain."

Michinaga was considered unlikely to ascend high in government. The office he had been given by his father was not at the loftiest level, and he possessed two talented elder brothers who had been appointed to more elevated posts. His brothers' sons and sons-in-law might eventually surpass him as well, for the brothers would see to such advancement. But Michinaga's astute political skills, combined with extraordinary luck—or what he and his Buddhist contemporaries called karma—would carry him to the top.

An individual's karma, in Buddhist theology, was determined by events that had happened not only in the present life but during previous incarnations as well. A lowly government position or a lover's rejection could be the result of something that had occurred in a former life. The belief in karma was pervasive. Writing about an excursion to see a cuckoo bird and the surprising failure of the court ladies to produce any poetry concerning the expedition, Sei Shonagon observed with some amusement, "Poetry seemed to be having bad karma that day."

There was nothing wrong with Michinaga's karma. Around 995, a smallpox epidemic swept through the capital, carrying off numerous palace officials, including Michinaga's eldest brother. Coincidentally, the other older brother died during this same period, probably from diabetes. Suddenly the way to Japan's highest office, the regency, lay open before Michinaga. He had one rival, however—his nephew Korechika, the former regent. Placed in a senior office when he was only 20 years old, Korechika believed he was entitled to fill the void left in the imperial hierarchy.

A man of charm and taste, who could sit up all night discussing literature with the emperor, Korechika had assumed control of the affairs of state during the last month of his father's illness. Although a temporary measure, it could have been the key to his future elevation. But Korechika had, in the eyes of some courtiers, abused his position by a display of arrogance, dismissing certain officials and issuing decrees that regulated the lengths of trousers and hunting robes. Yet Korechika was a favorite of his sister, the young empress Teishi, and was well liked by Emperor Ichijo, who was inclined to make his brother-in-law regent. But the emperor's mother, Grand Empress Senshi, supported Michinaga, her younger brother, who as the senior family member would traditionally have been appointed to that office.

Reports reached Senshi that Korechika "seized every opportunity to malign her and Michinaga to Emperor Ichijo." This was a fatal mistake. Senshi was a popular woman who commanded a great deal of respect at court and wielded some power. This was not unusual for noblewomen. Even women of lesser status, if they were part of the aristocracy, had considerable independence and influence, not only because of their marriage potential but also because they could inherit property, a family's source of position and wealth. The women of the court, therefore, were often outspoken and possessed a substantial degree of influence over their husbands and sons. The grand empress

A HARMONIOUS BLEND OF BELIEFS

As 29-year-old Emperor Horikawa lay near death in the early 12th century, his attendants called on one spiritual resource after another to save his life. When two Buddhist priests could not help, the imperial aides brought in an exorcist to drive away evil demons from the ailing monarch's body. The emperor revived briefly, only to suffer a relapse a few days later. Frantically, his servants read from various Buddhist sutras, or texts, as a group of 12 Buddhist mountain ascetics prayed over him. In desperation, the emperor himself eventually cried out, "May the Ise Shrine help me," appealing to the Shinto sun goddess. Despite all these efforts, the emperor died.

Horikawa's appeal for help from practitioners of different beliefs was not an unusual one. The Japanese welcomed spiritual aid wherever they could find it, from their native Shinto to the imported Asian creeds of Buddhism, Daoism, and Confucianism. People readily mingled these religions with a vast array of beliefs in ghosts, demons, and divination.

Shinto pervaded Japanese spiritual life in the beginning. Believing all things in nature—such as the sea, mountains, rocks, and waterfalls—had their own vital forces, called *kami,* the early Japanese offered prayers of thanksgiving and devotion to these spirits, whose good graces they depended on. At simple outdoor shrines in

In Ise Bay off southern Japan, "wedded rocks" serve as a sacred gateway to a Shinto shrine. A straw rope, used to mark such sites, joins the rocks, while a symbolic entrance gate, or torii, stands atop the "husband" rock *(left).*

Waving fans and beating drums, peasants dance outside a rural Shinto shrine during annual summer festivities. Later, the peasants offered prayers of thanksgiving to the kami in hopes of receiving a bountiful rice crop in the fall. Shinto shrines were sites of entertainment and merriment as well as ritual and prayer.

beautiful natural surroundings, people left offerings for the kami and sought to please them with a round of festivities based on the yearly planting cycle.

Buddhism was a fully developed religion when it arrived in Japan, by way of China and Korea, in the mid-sixth century. It immediately appealed to the aristocracy and intelligentsia, who were drawn to its elaborate rituals, organized monastic order, written religious texts, and artistic tradition, all of which Shinto lacked. Under Buddhism's influence, Shinto began to develop its own teachings. It assembled its spirits into an ordered hierarchy of deities with the sun goddess at its head—and Japan's imperial family as her direct descendants.

Although the basic outlooks of Shinto and Buddhism were very different—the latter stressed that life on earth was filled with suffering—the two religions achieved a peaceful coexistence, each assimilating aspects of the other. Both had an abiding belief in the sacred nature of all living things, and Buddhism had become adept at accommodating local traditions as it spread across Asia. Japanese Buddhist theology paired the kami with Buddhist deities, and Shinto shrines were built within Buddhist temples. And although Buddhism became widespread in medieval Japan, Shinto cults continued to flourish.

In a 16th-century scroll painting, pilgrims take a ritual bath in a river before passing over the bridge and through the torii to enter the shrine at Ise *(upper left)*. Dedicated to the sun goddess, it is one of Shinto's most sacred sites.

Illustrating the mingling of religions, a 14th-century painting shows the Shinto war god, Hachiman, holding rosary beads and staff in his guise as a Buddhist monk. Takeshiuchi Sukune, legendary minister of state, sits at Hachiman's feet.

marched to the imperial apartment with Michinaga in tow to confront her son, the emperor. Leaving her brother in the anteroom, Senshi invaded the inner chamber. Michinaga waited anxiously. At last the grand empress emerged with a victorious smile. It was AD 995, and Michinaga had attained supreme power.

Korechika, still burning with ambition, soon brought about his own downfall after falling in love with a beautiful court attendant. An ex-emperor happened to take an interest in the attendant's sister and began paying visits to the household. Mistakenly believing he and the former emperor were wooing the same woman, Korechika took action. On a moonlit night, when the supposed rival was returning from a visit to his lady, a band of Korechika's followers loosed a hail of arrows at him. He survived the attack, but Korechika's career did not. When Korechika's involvement was discovered, Michinaga and Emperor Ichijo insisted upon the young lover's banishment from Kyoto for several months. For the moment, Michinaga stood unchallenged.

During much of the period when Michinaga was climbing toward Japan's highest office, Sei Shonagon was serving Teishi as a lady-in-waiting. Sei began recording "odd facts and stories" of court life that would one day be collected into a volume known as the *Pillow Book*. Such creative endeavors were not unusual among upper-class women; they wrote most of the Heian-era literature that was written in Japanese. (While men wrote poetry in Japanese, they favored Chinese for prose.) Sei's trenchant comments on court life delighted readers.

By the time Sei Shonagon entered imperial service, the noble class had grown so large that the government bureaucracy included far more officials than necessary. As a result, men worked less, enjoying almost as much leisure time as the women, and both sexes often indulged in games, outings, festivals, and love affairs. Sei Shonagon knew a great deal about love affairs, her poetic skill and wit making her so engaging that she had

many suitors. Although unmarried, she would not have been expected to abstain from love affairs, for to do so would lead people to suspect that she was possessed by an evil spirit. During the many conversations Sei Shonagon enjoyed with male admirers, she sat behind a *kicho,* or "curtain of state," typically a portable frame about six feet high, curtained with an opaque material. Of varying width, it was deployed to guard the females of a household from view. A man sitting on the other side of the kicho glimpsed little more than a colorful sleeve or train. To allow a man behind the screen was to invite a physical relationship.

There were other forms of entertainment as well. Noblemen liked to watch the young men of immense bulk who came in from the provinces to display their skills at sumo wrestling. The gentlemen themselves played a game where they kicked a leather ball to one another, trying to keep it in the air. In one recorded bout, they managed 260 such passes before the ball hit the ground. The players' uniforms, though not full dress, were the same elegant, silk robes and stiff lacquered headdresses they donned for court appearances. Meanwhile, the women avidly watched boat racing along the Kamo River in the warmer months and in the winter diverted themselves with various activities, such as packing snow into balls or silver bowls.

Indoor games included backgammon and go, the latter a board game played with black and white stones. In a separate pastime known as *rango,* women tried to balance as many go stones as they could on a single finger. The

Watched by spectators and fellow contestants, an archer takes careful aim before sending an arrow flying from his bow toward the target. Competitive activities helped break the tedium of court life and were part of the annual cycle of religious and secular observances.

gentry especially enjoyed parlor games of skill or cleverness. In one contest, prize songbirds raised at home were judged according to their song and plumage. Sometimes dividing into teams, one group of guests might make up riddles that the other had to decipher. Poetry contests could get tense, as a poetic reputation was particularly esteemed. People also exhibited plants they had cultivated or paintings, incense, or fans they had created.

As Sei Shonagon reported, a multitude of festivals and ceremonies regulated court life, some religious in origin, others derived from folk celebrations. The year began with a ceremony at which the emperor prayed for the blessings of heaven. Later, he consumed special foods and wine. In Japan, the first of the year fell somewhere between Europe's January 15 and February 15. The day was not fixed in relation to the Western calendar because Japan's year was based on approximately 12 lunations, or cycles of the moon, as opposed to the solar year used in the West. The result was a calendar year that was about 11 days shorter than the West's. At certain intervals a 13th month was added to synchronize the calendar and the seasons.

Sei Shonagon enjoyed one of the annual festivals, called Full-Moon Gruel. On this old folk holiday, special gruel was stirred with elder-wood sticks, which were then used to strike women hoping to conceive male children. By Sei Shonagon's time, it had evidently become a game for some. Clutching gruel sticks, Sei Shonagon and her friends sneaked about the house hoping to catch each other by surprise. "Each one," the writer noted, "is constantly looking over her shoulder to make sure that no one is stealing up on her. Yet the precautions are useless, for before long one of the women manages to score a hit."

Another event mentioned was the Festival of the Snake, when wine cups were sent floating along a garden stream. Whenever guests lifted a cup from the water, they had to compose a poem. On the last day of the year, the Devil Chase occurred. An attendant in a red skirt and gold mask made the rounds of the imperial complex, shooting arrows into the air to banish evil spirits.

For Sei Shonagon and her contemporaries, the world was populated by many ghosts and demons. Illness was seen as a possession by an evil spirit. After attending a successful exorcism for a sick girl, Sei Shonagon wrote, "The priest had brought the spirit under control and, having forced it to beg for mercy, he now dismissed it." In addition to exorcists, people also consulted practitioners of divination and prophecy to learn when to begin a project and when to stay home. The route that one traveled to a destination could be critical; circuitous paths were often preferred.

Intelligent, kind, and charming, the empress Teishi easily won Sei Shonagon's love and loyalty. But to Fujiwara Michinaga, Teishi was a political adversary with strong influence over the emperor. To displace Teishi—and through her Korechika, who might return one day to court—and strengthen the Fujiwara impe-

any remaining hope Korechika had for advancement was tied to the rise of this nephew.

With Shoshi's place secured, Michinaga could graciously encourage the emperor to invite Teishi and her children to the palace for a visit. Ichijo was delighted to see his beloved wife and children once again, but after Teishi returned home from her palace visit, she discovered to her dismay that she was pregnant. Away from the court, she felt isolated, and her loss of status seemed even greater now that she was with child. It was reported that she often "gazed vacantly into space, her mind filled with nostalgic recollections." Occasionally she wrote melancholy poems; one was about her husband: "If he has not forgotten / The vows that were made / All through the night / I should like to see the color / Of the yearning tears he sheds."

"*Her face and figure were more beautiful than I can say.*"

rial ties, Michinaga exploited his 11-year-old daughter, Shoshi. Michinaga saw to it that she became the imperial consort, then second wife a year later, thus cementing Michinaga's own hold over the young emperor.

"Her face and figure were more beautiful than I can say," remarked an admittedly partial observer of Shoshi, whose loveliness soon accomplished its objective. Shoshi was frequently invited to visit the imperial bedchamber when she came of age. The emperor, himself barely 20, remarked playfully that her youth embarrassed him: "I feel like an old man beside you."

Empress Teishi retired with her children to her family home, where her brother, Korechika, was a frequent visitor. Teishi's only son, Prince Atsuyasu, still a baby, might yet become emperor, and

Teishi, age 24, died in childbirth soon after. Korechika held her in his arms and sobbed. Though cremation was the more common form of disposing of the dead, Korechika built a tomb for Teishi in Kyoto and bore her there in a gilded carriage through the falling snow. That night, according to a contemporary, the emperor arrived and "mourned until dawn, his sleeves drenched with icy tears."

Empress Teishi was gone, but Michinaga's daughter Shoshi thrived, as did Michinaga's fortunes. In 1008 the empress and her attendants took up residence at Tsuchimikado mansion, where Michinaga usually resided when not at the palace. Shoshi had become pregnant, making her ritually unclean and thus unfit to live

STYLE AND SUBSTANCE

In the poetry of Heian Japan, the paper, ink, brush strokes, and words were equally important. Nowhere was this more evident than in the *Anthology of Poems by the Thirty-Six Immortal Poets*, said to have been created around AD 1112. A total of 6,438 poems were reproduced in the 38-volume set, beautifully set down in flowing kana, a Japanese script, by as many as 20 calligraphers. The anthology boasted 687 different types of paper and various forms of artistic accompaniment. Collages, such as the one at left, used up to five different papers, which were torn or cut, then joined. Painted images were added to some poems, though the renderings did not have to illustrate the poems directly.

The page shown here offers a subtle blend of paper colors and a painting of a wooded mountain with ducks flying overhead to create a melancholic atmosphere befitting the verses. In them, a famous poet discourages the overtures of a former suitor interested in reviving their relationship: "They give no thought / To the years that have passed / Those tiny birds on the shore, / Even were they to stay / How could they be worth seeing!"

in the same building as the emperor. The mansion, or *shinden*, was a complex of wooden buildings with verandas—raised several feet from the ground on wooden pilings to better withstand humidity—linked in a rectangular form by roofed corridors and set among gardens and courtyards. The carefully landscaped garden with its hills and rocks displayed numerous well-cared-for plantings, some bent into interesting shapes. An artificial lake was fed by winding streams that flowed under the buildings.

Each major building held a large room, with partitions dividing it into smaller spaces as necessary. It was entered by a sliding or swinging door. Straw mats and cushions for seating dotted the bare wooden floors. The rooms, decorated in subdued colors, were sparsely furnished, but almost every piece in them was a work of art. There were chests of sandalwood, lacquered in gold or inlaid with mother-of-pearl; exquisite screens, painted by the best artists; and a round brazier of lacquered wood to provide heat.

Away from the living quarters were small huts, built above latrines dug into the earth. There was also a two-room bathhouse. In one room a huge iron pot of water stood boiling over a hearth. The steam it produced was drawn through a bamboo pipe into the next room, where the bathers sat, either to take a steam bath or in preparation for a dip in a large wooden tub of hot water. The shinden occupied several acres of land and provided plenty of comfort for the empress and her ladies-in-waiting.

Among Shoshi's ladies was Murasaki Shikibu, who came from a family of outstanding poets and scholars. She had entered imperial service after her husband died, and she found that attending the empress brought a satisfying relief from loneliness. In Murasaki's *Tale of Genji,* the title character, known as the Shining Prince, embodies the values of the Heian age and is said to be a composite of Michinaga and Korechika, though the novel is set about 75 years before their time.

Settled into one of the curtained partitions that served as rooms for the attendants, Murasaki was awakened one morning even before the gong, which sounded each day at 4:00 a.m. She heard a "thunder of footsteps" as 20 monks marched over the elaborately wrought bridges arching over garden streams. "The rise and fall of the chant as each priest sets out to best his neighbor is awe-inspiring," Murasaki recorded in her diary. She lay huddled in her bedchamber, known as a curtain dais, a nine-foot-square, black wooden platform, about two feet high, strewn with cushions. Four pillars

With its upturned tile roofs, Phoenix Hall, named for the two bronze birds on the peak of the central roof, appears to hover above the water's edge. Fujiwara Michinaga's son and successor, Yorimichi, built this stunning example of Heian architecture in the 1070s as a private chapel on an estate once owned by his father.

stood at each corner, and a frame with curtains surrounded the platform. Suspended from one pillar were two mirrors to keep away evil spirits.

Eventually Murasaki rose. She was almost as fully dressed as before she had retired, for it was customary for both men and women to sleep in their robes. The upper halves of the heavy, latticed shutters used during winter nights had already been raised that morning, leaving the three-foot-high lower shutters in place to separate her room from the veranda. Behind them were bamboo blinds, lowered to the top of the lower shutters. She rolled them up, peering into "the light morning mist." Michinaga was already at work, "ordering his attendants to clear the stream of some obstruction." Hearing the lady-in-waiting, Michinaga plucked a maiden flower and tossed it over her partition. "And where's the reply?" he asked.

Murasaki moved without hesitation to her inkstone, into which she dipped her brush and drafted her answer: "Now I see / This lovely maiden flower / In bloom, / I know for certain / That the dew discriminates."

Michinaga smiled. "Quick, aren't we?" he said and borrowed her brush to write an answering verse: "The morning dew / Does not discriminate; / The maiden flower / Takes on the colors / That it pleases."

Custom and courtesy required Murasaki and Michinaga to reply promptly to a poem with another in a similar vein. To be unable to dash off well-written verse at a moment's notice was to be virtually tongue-tied. The typical short poem, or waka, was restricted to a mere 31 syllables, and expressed ideas or hinted at meanings by the use of subtle wordplay, allusions to famous earlier verses, and pleasing sound and rhythm.

If Murasaki enjoyed Michinaga's poetry and banter, it is not clear how she felt about his other overtures. One night she was awakened by a tapping on her shutters, the signal of a gentleman caller. Murasaki "lay awake all night without making a sound." The next morning her nighttime caller, Michinaga, was revealed

in a poem handed to her: "How sad for him who stands the whole night long / Knocking on your cedar door / Tap-tap-tap like the cry of the kuina bird." She answered: "Sadder for her who had answered the kuina's tap, / For it was no innocent bird who stood there knocking on the door."

There were other events besides flirtations to record during the stay at Tsuchimikado mansion. One night, Murasaki awakened "to a scene of great bustle and noise." A number of courtiers were busily rearranging the furnishings in the empress's apartment. The curtains, cushions, and mats of the empress's bedchamber were being exchanged for a new set, all in white. Shoshi was in labor.

The ladies-in-waiting, dressed in white, streamed in to fill the room and prepared to sit there until the baby was born. Exorcists and diviners arrived, as well as Buddhist bishops and archbishops from the great temples in the land to augment the ranks of the spell-chanting priests. Courtiers and priests crammed into a narrow space just outside the imperial dais. Murasaki reported that "everyone lost the hems of their trains and their sleeves in the crush."

Suddenly, amidst the anguished waiting, "they started to shave Her Majesty's head and made her take her vows." These were religious precautions taken in case something should go amiss. From time to time the men threw rice upon the heads of the ladies-in-waiting, a gesture meant to ward off evil spirits; it served to release the tension for a few moments. At last the empress gave birth, and the priestly wailing rose to a crescendo. Michinaga sent a messenger to the palace to inform the emperor of the safe birth of his second son, Atsuhira, who would eventually become Emperor Go-Ichijo. The empress's mother performed the ceremony of cutting the umbilical cord. Murasaki wrote, "It was midday, yet we all felt just as though the morning sun had risen into a cloudless sky."

The days that followed were marked by ceremony, such as the ritual of the first bath, which took place by torchlight on the veranda of the main building about six the first evening. Servants brought jars of hot water, while four scribes carried in the bathtub. They passed the bathing equipment to the ladies-in-waiting, who poured the water into the tub and supervised the bathing. A Buddhist archbishop blessed the bath.

"Pretty yet shy, shrinking from sight, unsociable, fond of old tales . . . , such is the unpleasant opinion that people have of me," wrote Murasaki Shikibu, pictured at her desk on a fan painted in 1630. A lady-in-waiting to an empress, Murasaki used her intimate knowledge of the court and the lives of its aristocrats to create her famous novel *The Tale of Genji*.

Elated, Michinaga entered, proudly bearing the baby. The celebrations and rituals continued for eight days. Gifts, distributed by Michinaga, included robes, bedclothes, and rolls of silk. Meanwhile, Michinaga made sure that everything in the mansion was repaired and polished in anticipation of the emperor's first visit to his newborn son. Even the gardens were refurbished; "rare chrysanthemums were sought and transplanted," to be arranged in attractive patterns according to hue.

Clothing and personal appearance during the entire proceeding were as important as ever, and everyone sought to distinguish themselves in some way. Although all were required to wear white and dress simply, they had decorated their jacket cuffs and embroidered their trains, some using silver threads or, as Murasaki related, "inlaid pearl to

Leaning against her cushion and, like her attendants, dressed in the ritual white clothing of childbirth, an expectant mother waits to give birth. In the adjoining room two Buddhist monks and a mountain ascetic chant prayers, while outside a kneeling priest and two other men pray and an archer wards off evil spirits. Birth, like many aspects of Heian life, was highly ritualized.

an absurd degree." Others had silver foil inlaid into the patterns on their fans and adorned their hair with hairpins and white ribbons. Apparently, without color combinations to distinguish them, women were distressed by the basic similarity of their garb. Describing the ending of the week of ritual, Murasaki no doubt pinpointed what was uppermost in the minds of many: "On the eighth day, everyone changed back into their colored robes."

Michinaga had the baby, Prince Atsuhira, named as an heir to the throne, displacing Teishi's son. Korechika's hopes for advancement through his nephew lay in ruins. But further troubles loomed: Rumors began circulating that Korechika and his supporters had placed curses on the new prince as well as on Empress Shoshi and Michinaga. Though some observers blamed Michinaga himself for spreading these accusations, the damage to Korechika was done. He was again banished from the court and died in disgrace not long after.

Further strengthening his family's position, Michinaga arranged for his eldest son, Yorimichi, to marry the granddaughter of a former emperor. The wedding ceremony was a splendid affair, the lovely bride arriving with a host of attendants, including 20 ladies-in-waiting. Two nights later, the bridal couple celebrated the ancient ritual known as the Third Night Rice Cakes. The bride and groom, huddled in a curtained bed in the bride's home, awaited the arrival of her mother, who pushed aside the curtains and "discovered" the two lovers. She then insisted that Yorimichi eat three rice cakes cooked over the household fire, which symbolized that he was now part of the family. The groom then donned a suit of clothes given him by his new in-laws and joined all of his wife's relatives in a great feast.

Having made a brilliant match for his son as well as having maneuvered his daughter Shoshi into the rank of empress, Michinaga now sought to solidify his family's position by marrying his second daughter, Kenshi, to his nephew, the present crown prince and heir to the throne ahead of grandson Atsuhi-ra. In AD 1011 Emperor Ichijo abdicated, and the crown prince ascended the throne as Emperor Sanjo. Kenshi was now empress, and young Atsuhira became crown prince.

But Sanjo, in his mid-thirties, was not as easily manipulated as a boy emperor. For four years he and Michinaga struggled for control. At last, debilitated by weakening eyesight, Sanjo was persuaded to abdicate. Michinaga's grandson was crowned Emperor Go-Ichijo, and Michinaga married his third daughter, Ishi, to the new emperor, her nephew. Exhilarated by all his accomplishments, he wrote: "I cannot help but feel / That the full moon / Will never wane, / This world is truly / Mine alone."

That same year Michinaga placed the regency in the hands of his son, Yorimichi, and retired to become a Buddhist monk. Ex-emperors and other high officials often turned to the priesthood. They did not always retire to a cloister, however, remaining active in Kyoto society. Nor was their power or influence diminished. Yorimichi served as regent for 50 years, but for as long as his father lived, it was Michinaga who was ruler of Japan.

Michinaga achieved the pinnacle of governmental power for the Fujiwara and expected to leave that legacy to his descendants. But the decline of the imperial landownership system that had led to aristocratic wealth would soon threaten to topple the Heian court and the Fujiwara regency with it.

By the end of the 10th century, powerful clans like the Fujiwara had expanded their holdings into vast estates known as *shoen,* many of them completely autonomous from the state. A top-ranking official might live off the labor of the many peasant families farming his lands, while he paid nothing to the state and the state had no control over his estate's administration. The imperial court's financial resources and legal power over its subjects deteriorated. The courtiers thus helped undermine the powers of the government that had ensured their own ascendancy.

Snugly ensconced in their beloved capital, the highest patricians seldom if ever visited the land that supported them. Little understanding or sympathy was expressed for the men and women who made a life of luxury possible. Outside of Kyoto, country life presented a decided contrast to the studied elegance of the capital. Rice was harvested wherever possible, from swamps and river deltas to forests and uplands. A majority of Japan's population were illiterate peasants who toiled in the rice fields, returning to crude wooden huts, where they lived off a fraction of the crop they themselves had raised. They lived in small villages with at least one temple, surrounded by agricultural lands.

The villagers' dress was simple, with women in *kosodes* (early kimonos), which were often worn singly in the summer, and men in smocks over a pair of trousers. In summer the women worked in the fields in trousers like the men. In the winter, people wore loose cloaks as well, which in colder regions were usually fitted with hoods. Garments were colored indigo, violet, or dark red, using common plant dyes. Men and women wore wooden clogs or straw sandals without socks or, in snowy regions, boots made of plaited straw.

In the countryside bandits were a danger, and peasants cultivating small plots of land often were forced to seek the protection of larger landowners. The small cultivators

Two women talk at the threshold of a peasant hut while the family next door looks on. Farther down the road, women go about their daily chores, hauling water, stamping laundry to clean it, and tending their gardens. Peasants in Heian Japan suffered under the burden of heavy taxes as well as strict court edicts.

would commend their plots to larger owners in exchange for physical protection and exemption from taxes. The peasant farmer would continue to grow rice on the land but would give a percentage of it to the overlord. Clans increased their shoen by this method as well as by claiming and cultivating land not previously used for rice. As the number and size of shoen gradually increased, private landowners had to hire bands of fighting men to protect their property and lives. This need for protection spurred the growth of a class of expert fighters, known as samurai. While these warriors worked for the proprietors, they also entered into battle for the sake of their own honor and to gain power for their families. The samurai's honor was demonstrated by absolute loyalty to his overlord.

Leaders of the warrior bands were often officials from Kyoto who had settled in the provinces or the younger sons of noble families. By the late 11th century, most of these fighting men had allied themselves with one of two powerful warrior

families, the Minamoto, also called Genji, and the Taira, also called Heike. Both clans claimed descent from past emperors. They shared common interests—the desire to protect their lands and avoid taxation by Kyoto—but they competed with each other for control of the countryside.

By the 12th century, the Fujiwara were struggling to retain their dominance, challenged by a series of retired emperors, each of whom, upon leaving imperial office, kept his own court. Their self-proclaimed "retirement" relieved them from ritual duties while allowing them to keep control by manipulating the reigning emperor, usually a son or grandson, in competition with the Fujiwara regents.

In 1156 a Fujiwara leader allied himself with one emperor's son to challenge the designated heir. To support his own position, the imperial heir enlisted the backing of both Yoshitomo, head of the Minamoto warrior clan, and Kiyomori, leader of the Taira. The heir's victory ended the Fujiwara era, but it set in

Hungry ghosts *(below)*, punished for their excesses in life, hover around people who pour libations on ancestor monuments before joining the throng at a crowded temple gate *(opposite)*. As the Heian era came to a close, such grim images of life abounded.

was allowed to remain with his mother for a few years before being sent to a northern monastery. Another of Yoshitomo's sons whose life was spared by Kiyomori was Yoritomo, who was exiled to eastern Japan. Kiyomori's uncharacteristic acts of mercy would bear bitter fruit in later years.

Kiyomori became the de facto ruler of Japan. He saw little need to replace the many Fujiwara ministers who still governed and who had suffered little from the wars in the countryside. Now, however, members of the Taira were also appointed to important positions in the Kyoto government and the outlying areas.

Kiyomori treated the emperor as a figurehead, in the manner of the Fujiwara. He even married one of his daughters to the emperor. Later he forced his son-in-law to abdicate in favor of his infant grandson, Antoku. With Kyoto at their feet, the Taira became arrogant and could be heard throughout the capital, making comments such as "not to be a Taira is not to be a man!"

In the long run, however, this government made the same mistakes as its predecessors. Taira nobles grew preoccupied with life in Kyoto while, in the provinces, the Minamoto regrouped under the leadership of Yoritomo, who had been spared as a boy by Kiyomori. Yoritomo's warriors began to challenge Taira strongholds. In 1181 the aged Kiyomori died. Two years later, Minamoto forces, led by a cousin of Yoritomo named Yoshinaka, reached Kyoto and forced the Taira from the capital. But the retreating armies took with them the emperor Antoku. Although still a child, Antoku was important as a symbol, legitimizing the Taira even as they fled.

An ex-emperor now entered the fray, conspiring with Yoshinaka to overthrow his cousin Yoritomo, who was still the leader

motion a series of events that would weaken his rule. Now the Taira and Minamoto leaders saw how they might control royal politics using military might and soon ended their short-lived collaboration. In 1160 a brief but fierce contest occurred, in which the Minamoto leader, Yoshitomo, was forced to retreat. He was subsequently murdered, betrayed by one of his own men.

Many legends surround Kiyomori's rise to power, including the story that Kiyomori fell in love with his former enemy's consort, the beautiful Tokiwa, mother of one of Yoshitomo's sons. Tokiwa bargained with Kiyomori, agreeing to become his mistress in exchange for the life of her young son, Yoshitsune, who

of the Minamoto. Meanwhile, Yoritomo had established a stronghold in Kamakura, located about 300 miles east from Kyoto, a good two weeks' journey. He issued a decree stating that all the Minamoto owed their allegiance to him and were forbidden to take orders from the court. To eliminate the threat posed by his cousin, Yoritomo enlisted the help of his younger half brother, Yoshitsune, who had fought tirelessly against the Taira.

Yoshitsune was a superb military leader, who would become a Japanese folk hero. His slight build established him as an underdog in the Japanese imagination. After being banished to a monastery as a baby, one fantastic tale claimed he learned to use a sword from a long-nosed goblin who lived in the woods near his place of exile. Unaware, the legend goes, of his real identity, Yoshitsune discovered the truth one day in a genealogy of the Minamoto clan and from then on was obsessed with the idea of avenging his father's death.

Yoshitsune forced Yoshinaka's forces out of Kyoto, and Yoshinaka was killed, fleeing with his few remaining supporters. Fighting one heroic battle after another, Yoshitsune finally drove the Taira into the sea off Kyushu. Yoshitsune commandeered enough boats to pursue them. In the conflict, many of the faithful Taira drowned, along with the young emperor Antoku.

The court of the new emperor, half brother of the slain Antoku, immediately acclaimed Yoshitsune for his victory, even before congratulating the supreme commander, Yoritomo. Alarmed by the favoritism shown his charismatic brother, the Minamoto leader—who could

afford no possible rival as he sought to stabilize his new government—refused to see Yoshitsune when he arrived at Kamakura to turn over several prisoners of war. Yoshitsune wrote a moving plea for his brother's sympathy, but it was rejected. Forced by his brother to become a fugitive, Yoshitsune was hunted mercilessly until he finally killed himself, his wife, and his child.

Yoritomo now had no rival, but he was seen as a cold and ruthless leader. His followers shuddered at his harshness as, for example, on a day when a vassal arrived bearing the head of his master, who had plotted against Yoritomo. The ruler had the vassal himself beheaded, reasoning that anyone who betrayed his master could not be trusted.

Yoritomo established his *bakufu*, or "tent government," in his old stronghold of Kamakura, far from the corruption of Kyoto. From there he controlled the provincial forces that had been neglected by his predecessors. All other warlords owed him absolute obedience and were expected to contribute to his government, as needed. Besides the regular rice duties, they might be called upon to provide timber for his building projects, donate horses to his mounted forces, or lend him attendants when he traveled.

Backed by this military might, he could dictate from Kamakura the actions of the emperor's government in Kyoto, which had little force to counter him. He had the emperor grant him the power to appoint stewards, land managers who effectively controlled the wealth from the estates. This gave Yoritomo dominance over civil affairs

Fire rages through Kyoto's imperial palace in 1160 as the rebel forces of Minamoto Yoshitomo attempt to slay those loyal to the emperor, including the Taira family and its leader, Kiyomori. Although the rebels abducted the emperor, he eventually escaped, and Yoshitomo was killed.

Though Kiyomori reigned for two decades, the Minamoto finally defeated the Taira in 1185. The ruthless leader Minamoto Yoritomo, seen at right in ceremonial robes, ended 400 years of rule centered on the court in Kyoto to become shogun of Japan.

throughout the provinces. By developing an efficient bureaucracy, he reinforced his political power. He organized his Kamakura government to include an administrative council, a court system, and a directorate for dealing with military affairs. His courts operated efficiently and fairly, settling disputes between various lords with surprisingly little bloodshed. As Japan's most powerful leader, he took the title *seii-taishogun*—meaning "barbarian-suppressing commander in chief"—but was more simply referred to as shogun.

The spartan bakufu government shunned the pomp and ceremony that had been the hallmark of the Kyoto nobles. In spite of his disdain for grandeur, however, Yoritomo traveled in style. A contemporary described his entry into Kyoto: "Over 700 horsemen preceded him, and more than 300 were grouped behind him. Riding a black horse, and wearing an apron of deer's summer fur over a glossy tri-colored robe of dark blue, light blue, and red, he was an impressive figure."

Yoritomo's rule ended abruptly when he fell from his horse and died in 1199. Legend had it that this fall was caused by the ghost of his brother, Yoshitsune. The stability that he had engendered did not last. Following his death, his 18-year-old son became shogun, but this young man was soon forced out of office and then murdered, allegedly by his mother's family, the Hojo. A second son became shogun, only to be murdered as well. The power of the shogun eventually shifted to a shogunal regent who was a member of the Hojo family. The Hojo then exercised authority by controlling various child shoguns, replicating the old Fujiwara methods.

The gracious example of Kyoto proved irresistibly appealing for the shoguns, and eventually they too cultivated a court society. As a result, the austere character of life at Kamakura eroded, along with its authority, for Kyoto mustered forces to challenge the bakufu regime, as did various warrior groups. A century later, Japan erupted anew into conspiracy and armed conflict.

Heian Courtship and Marriage

Just as the Fujiwara gained power by marrying their daughters into the royal family, the young men of Kyoto's courtier class could seek wealth, prestige, and political advantage in their own marital alliances. A wife would bring her family's property with her into the marriage, and her father often played a large part in the advancement of his son-in-law's career.

Although many Heian men were monogamous, it was not unusual for a man to take several wives or lovers, and society recognized principal marriages, secondary wives or concubines, and casual love affairs. But these distinctions could change: A first marriage, arranged by parents, might be considered the principal marriage, but so might a second or third. Sometimes, the only way to tell was by which son became his father's heir.

A romanticized version of Heian courtship and marriage was set down by Murasaki Shikibu, a woman of the court and author of the literary classic *The Tale of Genji*. Illustrated in paintings from 12th-century scrolls, shown here and on the following pages, the tale offers a glimpse into the era's world of romance, but also reveals the jealousies and sorrow that attended these relationships.

A husband attempts to console his wife with music from his lute after she has discovered he has taken another wife. Jealousies flared frequently in Heian Japan, where men could have a number of spouses, divorce was easy, and both sexes pursued casual love affairs.

Two aristocrats look at the illustrations from one of the romantic novels popular with women of the upper class while one lady-in-waiting reads from the text and another combs out her mistress's freshly washed hair. Literacy and a talent for music and calligraphy enhanced a woman's prestige—and her appeal to the opposite sex.

Courtship behind the Curtain

Whether a man was looking for a wife or a concubine, Heian courting rituals held fast. Informed about a possible intended by a matchmaker or friend, a suitor professed his interest by first sending the woman a sentimental poem. Her reply was examined carefully for its calligraphy and poetic skill. Although many considered long, luxuriant hair the hallmark of beauty, often it was a lady's handwriting or her way with words that first won a man's affections.

If the lady was willing and the gentleman impressed, he arranged to visit her. Their meeting took place at night behind her curtain of state, where their amorous adventures—fully sanctioned by convention and the woman's parents—lasted until just before daybreak. If the man wished to see her again, he hastened home to compose a "next morning" letter, a sign that all had gone well. The woman could, if she wished, fend him off with polite badinage. But if both agreed, he visited a second time and then a third. After the third visit, which was viewed as a sign of commitment, the suitor would be allowed to stay past the dawn.

"First you must study penmanship. Next you must learn to play the seven-string zither better than anyone else. And also you must memorize all the poems in the twenty books of the Kokin Shu."

After their third evening of love behind a screen and silk curtain designed for a woman's privacy, a courting couple see each other for the first time in daylight.

Marital Arrangements

Though courtship could be a matter of the heart, it typically was an arranged affair among the Heian aristocracy. Usually, the bridegroom's family chose a suitable woman from an equal or higher social class to wed their young man. But in the case of an emperor's daughters, it was the reverse: The royal family chose the husband. In those cases, the bridegroom's political and economic future outweighed his present social status. In many of these arranged marriages, the wedding took place when the bride and groom were in their early teens.

Since children this young could not manage their own domestic affairs, the couple would live in the home of the wife's family. But this was often true, as well, when the partners were older. In the Heian era, houses frequently were passed on from mothers to daughters, and even when a husband would build a house for himself and his wife, he might put the title in her name.

The ownership of property was important for women. Not only was it a major component of her favorable prospects for marriage, it also helped to provide some security for her and her offspring should she lose her husband later to death or divorce.

"There is something I might wager,"

said the emperor, alluding to his eligible

daughters, "but I am not quite sure

that I have the courage."

> ## *"To keep many ladies*
> ## *is to suffer*
> ## *many troubles."*

A wife creeps up behind her husband as he reads a letter from the mother of another woman he's been pursuing. Similar scenes between husbands and wives may have happened fairly often among the more sexually adventurous Heian aristocrats.

Jealousy and Intrigue

As one might suspect, polygamy and love affairs created tension in Heian households. A concubine or lover—unless she was a favorite of the gentleman—feared being cast aside and left penniless. A wife, though assured of her status, could not relax either. She fretted about her children's future, for her husband could decide to pass over his legitimate offspring and give preference to his other children.

Since women could also take lovers, jealousy was common to both sexes. But women, whose servants watched after the children and performed all of the household duties, had fewer opportunities to mitigate its torment. They rarely left their homes and were expected to keep feelings of ill will to themselves. Although some vented their anger at their husbands, most felt that since infidelity was inevitable, it was best to endure their jealousy "in silence like other women."

Prince Genji, head bowed in sorrow, cradles his wife's son by another man. For the baby's sake, Genji pretends that the child is his own. The red trays, partially hidden by a bamboo screen, contain the traditional dishes of rice offered upon the birth of a nobleman's son.

CHAPTER TWO

Swords of the Samurai

Dressed in black and red armor and a helmet with fearsome horns, a mounted samurai is ready for battle, with a long sword on his left side, a short sword on his right, and a deadly *naginata* (a polearm with a long blade) clutched in his hand. Samurai and other warriors fought on behalf of warlords in their battles for control of Japan that lasted almost continuously for four centuries.

During the autumn of 1274, Takezaki Suenaga rode hard for Hakata Bay on the northwest coast of the island of Kyushu. A large armada of invaders from China and Korea was reportedly headed for the coast, intent on forcing the Japanese to bow to the rule of Khubilai Khan. Since 1268 the Mongol emperor of northern China had been attempting, through a series of thinly veiled threats, to institute the kind of lord-vassal hegemony over Japan that he was establishing over Korea and other neighboring nations. His first message addressed the Japanese emperor insultingly as "the ruler of a small country." Though much of Japanese culture and technology derived from the Chinese, Japan for centuries had refused to submit to the tributary relationship demanded by imperial China. After six years of what he considered subtle prodding, Khubilai had evidently decided that Japan needed more forceful persuasion.

In early November 1274, word had reached Suenaga's province in southern Kyushu that two small Japanese islands to the northwest of Kyushu, Tsushima and Iki, had fallen to a Mongol-Chinese invasion force. The Japanese had been badly outnumbered. According to traditional accounts—always somewhat suspect in their estimation of troops or casualties in war—the invading Mongol and Chinese army, which had sailed from southern Korea in nearly 800 vessels built and manned by Koreans, was 15,000 strong. The defenders of Tsushima and Iki were estimated at only a few hundred. Fighting heroically to the last man, the Japanese warriors were horrified by the invaders' indiscriminate killing of women, children, and other noncombatants. But to the Mongols, visiting terror upon civilians was simply another weapon of war.

Hearing that these barbaric invaders were now headed toward Kyushu's Hakata Bay, Suenaga and other warriors prepared for battle. The most aristocratic among them blackened their teeth, applied powder and perfume, and carefully tucked their hair into a topknot. Japanese warriors who lost at battle were typically beheaded, and meticulous grooming ensured that even in death their dignity was intact. The fighters then gathered their weapons—a bow, a dagger, and one or two swords. They also tucked into the gear a deerskin, typically used to sit upon or hold one's place during archery practice. In war, the skin served as a seat for a warrior about to be executed.

These were the traditional preparations of the samurai, as the professional warriors who could trace their roots to old clan aristocracy were known. The name, meaning "those who serve," had earlier been applied to personal attendants, and samurai still acted as trusted retainers. A warrior's first loyalties were to his immediate overlord, and it was his duty to die for that lord if necessary—even if by his own hand to avoid capture or to atone for an unworthy act. In exchange for loyal service to the landowners who hired the men for their private armies, the warriors received grants of land or the right to be stewards of small estates.

The samurai adhered to a code of behavior—later known as bushido, or the way of the warrior—that demanded physical hardship, absolute devotion to duty, and bravery in all things. The code represented the ideal, of course. Treachery and cowardice also existed in the ranks of the samurai, and some had misgivings about taking lives for a living. It was not unheard of for an elite warrior to retire to a monastery to pray for the souls of those he had slain.

Like others of his kind, Suenaga had probably apprenticed to a master in archery and swordsmanship and endured such hardships as extended fasts and barefoot marches through the snow. He also may have been a devotee of Zen, a form of Buddhism imported from China. Japan's military rulers had largely embraced Zen because of its emphasis on discipline and on focusing the mind. Before he departed for Hakata Bay, Suenaga had certainly prayed at the

Samurai Takezaki Suenaga charges toward the Mongol invaders sent by Khubilai Khan in 1274 to subdue Japan. Even though his horse has been fatally wounded and his helmet pierced by an arrow, Suenaga hurls himself at the enemy, ignoring the flames from an exploding bomb flying overhead. This scene appears on a scroll commissioned by Suenaga to commemorate his adventures in battle.

local Shinto shrine or Buddhist temple, imploring the various deities to permit him to distinguish himself in the coming battle.

On November 18 the Mongols anchored in Hakata Bay. When they began to land troops the next day, they found themselves facing several thousand Japanese warriors, Suenaga and five followers among them. The defenders engaged the invaders at several points around the bay. At its initial position, Suenaga's little band of five was dwarfed by much larger groups of 100 or more Japanese brought by higher-ranking warriors with large estates. Suenaga decided to head to the port city of Hakata, which was also under attack, hoping to achieve greater glory there. This was typical of samurai warriors, who liked to take the initiative in battle in order to reap special rewards. Once again there were many fighters already in position when he arrived, and he and his

followers chose a third location. There, at last, Suenaga joined forces with a powerful warrior from his own province who was pushing hard against the invaders.

The samurai launched their assault in the time-honored manner. An arrow with a humming or whistling head was fired to signal the start of the battle. Then, one by one, the samurai rode forward to seek out individual enemy warriors of comparable rank for man-to-man combat. Traditionally, a warrior found his match by loudly announcing his family lineage and its credentials, concluding perhaps on a note of false humility in which he disparaged his own ability. Once paired off with an opponent, he usually used his sword to try to stun (dealing a mortal blow from horseback was difficult) and unseat the foe. Then he dismounted, delivered the kill with a short dagger he wore on his waist, and finally slashed off his opponent's head. Heads would be counted after the battle and then taken to the overlord as trophies and as proof of the kill.

To their dismay, however, Suenaga and the other samurai quickly discovered that this was not at all how the Mongols fought. The enemy used the group tactics perfected over the past half-century in the vast Mongol conquests over Asia. Highly disciplined groups of archers and spearmen executed precise maneuvers to commands relayed by drums. The first samurai who advanced to challenge the foe to one-on-one combat found himself dodging barrages of poison-tipped arrows. Then he was surrounded and massacred. The samurai had never encountered such superior firepower. The short, powerful Mongol bows were effective at up to 240 yards, twice the range of the Japanese longbows. And for the first time the Japanese faced gunpowder in the form of catapult-launched projectiles that exploded with a deafening bang, frightening the samurai's horses and burning both the beasts and their riders.

Against these unfamiliar tactics and terrifying weapons, Suenaga and his men fought with all the unmatched courage of the proud

SAMURAI ARMS AND EQUIPMENT

In the Heian period, samurai started out as mounted archers who carried swords. During a duel, two warriors would gallop past each other firing arrows. As the feudal period advanced, the samurai relied less on bows and more on swords as they fought on foot more frequently—partly the result of 14th-century battles waged in hilly and wooded terrain. And as samurai warfare changed, so did body armor.

Heian samurai wore the *oyoroi* (great harness), a boxlike sheath with a paneled skirt that hung from the shoulders with broad straps and fastened around the waist.

The armor was composed of horizontal rows of lacquered iron or leather, laced together with braided silk cord. Large rectangular shoulder guards acted as shields against arrow attacks, while a fabric sleeve sewn with armor plates protected the outstretched bow arm (usually the left) from shoulder to fingertip. The other arm remained unencumbered for drawing the bow. Shin guards protected the lower legs.

Samurai on foot needed more flexible protection. They wore wraparound body armor—called *domaru* or *haramaki*—that fastened on the side or in the back. Though still composed of iron plates, it weighed far less than armor for mounted warriors. Shin guards were lengthened to protect the knees, and thigh guards were added, while both arms sported sleeves of lacquered chain mail.

Both Heian and feudal helmets were made of riveted iron plates with hanging guards for the neck and shoulders. Further protection came from a face mask, which usually covered the brow and cheeks of the Heian warriors and the cheeks, chin, and nose of later fighters. The latter also benefited from innovative throat guards that helped defend against decapitation.

A samurai dons thigh guards over layers of padding—robe, pantaloons, and shin guards—tying the sash around his waist like an apron.

The warrior fastens the straps of his torso armor, which includes shoulder flaps and a split skirt for easy movement.

Shoulder guards and sword on, the samurai secures his face mask and throat protector over a cotton skullcap worn to cushion his iron helmet.

A samurai's greatest protection, however, lay with his weapons. Heian samurai wore swords suspended by cords, while later fighters thrust theirs into a sash. Warriors also carried short daggers, or *tanto*, into battle. Whatever the period, dressing for battle was a time-consuming exercise, as seen on the previous page in illustrations from a manual entitled *Essentials for the Mounted Warrior.*

Samurai embellished their weapons as well as their armor with decorative patterns, added gilded metalwork and copper crests resembling animal antlers to helmets, and enlivened masks with imposing boar-hair mustaches or beards. A fully dressed and armed samurai was an impressive and intimidating sight, as the 18th-century set of armor on page 52 clearly shows.

The savagery of samurai combat is graphically depicted in this screen painting fragment from a 12th-century battle scene. A mounted warrior wrenches back the head of an enemy soldier and prepares to plunge a dagger into his opponent's throat.

The lacquered hilt of this gleaming 14th-century *tachi*, or long sword, is covered in the hardened skin of a ray, its grip wrapped with silk cord.

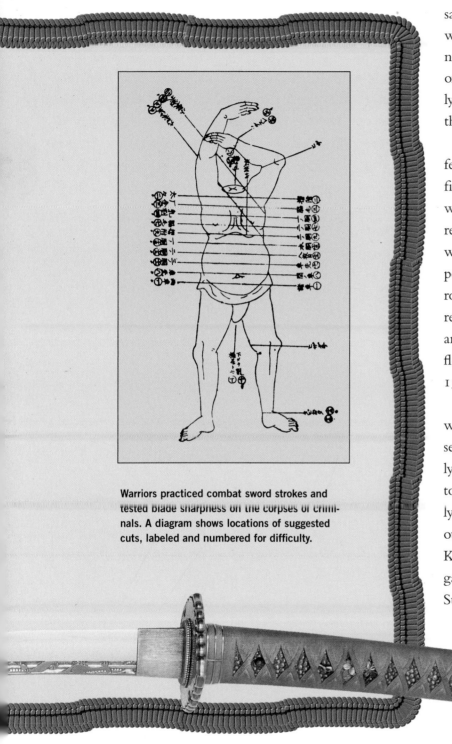

Warriors practiced combat sword strokes and tested blade sharpness on the corpses of criminals. A diagram shows locations of suggested cuts, labeled and numbered for difficulty.

samurai. Suenaga, gripping his sword with both hands, slashed one way and then another at the enemies engulfing him. Then Suenaga and three of his men lost their horses and stumbled about on foot, badly wounded. His entire group would almost certainly have been slaughtered but for the sudden appearance of more than a hundred of their countrymen.

As darkness fell, the battered Japanese defenders withdrew a few miles inland and took cover behind some defensive walls. A fierce storm began to stir during the night. While the surviving warriors lay there drenched and exhausted, awaiting the arrival of reinforcements from the main island of Honshu, the enemy also withdrew. The Korean boat pilots, fearing that the brewing tempest would wreck their vessels on the rocks of the bay and maroon the invasion force on land, talked the Mongol generals into reembarking their troops. By dawn, they had sailed out of the bay and into the teeth of a typhoon. Nearly a third of the Mongol fleet was lost, and according to a surviving record, an estimated 13,500 soldiers and sailors drowned.

After the failure of the enemy invasion, Suenaga and other warriors waited expectantly for the rewards for meritorious service that customarily followed a battle. Suenaga felt especially deserving. In contrast to some samurai who reportedly refused to fight or change locations to meet the invaders, he had eagerly engaged the enemy and had suffered wounds. Unlike previous battles against domestic opponents, however, the rulers in Kamakura, the military capital on the island of Honshu, had gained no land or other booty to distribute to the faithful. For Suenaga, this lack was all the more appalling because the responsible official in Kyushu had not even reported his valor to the *bakufu*—the military government. Suenaga considered this a serious loss of face.

In his desperation, Suenaga decided to travel to Kamakura to personally plead his case. It would be an arduous journey north from the south of Kyushu to the east-central coast of Honshu. Suenaga had no money for such a trip. But he was determined to win the recognition and rewards he deserved, and he sold some of his horses and saddles to fund the trip.

He left his home in June 1275, and nearly two months later, he reached Kamakura. A former fishing village, the city was now home to 50,000 residents. It was strategically placed—bounded on three sides by mountains and on the fourth by a bay. Suenaga entered through one of seven mountain passes, each of which was guarded by a control post. Here Suenaga saw houses built in tiers down the slopes of the surrounding hills. As another 13th-century visitor described it, the houses seemed "superimposed one upon another . . . looking just like things thrown pell-mell into a bag."

The samurai descended into the heart of the city, where the homes of the great warriors lined a broad avenue that led to the sea. The size of each of these residences was prescribed by the bakufu according to the social standing and means of the family. The bakufu tried to regulate the lives of the population in other ways as well. Two decades earlier, in 1252, the body had decided there was too much sake in town and had confiscated precisely 37,274 jars. One jar was allocated to each house or family and the rest was destroyed. Directives ordering that the streets be kept clean had less effect. Suenaga found the street corners littered with refuse and even dead horses. Most of the city's inhabitants were poor, and the many Zen Buddhist temples operated shelters to aid the sick and the orphaned.

Suenaga had plenty of opportunity to observe Kamakura and its environs. For nearly two months he was unsuccessful in gain-

ing an audience with an official of the bakufu. Finally, in October, Adachi Yasumori, chief of the military government's rewards office, agreed to see him. "I am not appealing merely because I want a reward," Suenaga told him. "If my claim to having fought in the vanguard be proved false, please cut off my head immediately. I have only one wish: for my merit to be known to the shogun."

Suenaga's persistence paid off. He was presented with a prize horse and appointed to the stewardship of an estate on his home island of Kyushu. Though many other warriors had also appealed directly to the bakufu, Suenaga was one of just 120 to receive a reward. He would never forget it.

One of Suenaga's arguments on his own behalf had been that a reward "would serve as a great encouragement in the event of another war." In fact, another invasion was coming. While Suenaga was in Kamakura pleading his case, Khubilai Khan summoned the Japanese emperor to his new court at present-day Beijing to pay him homage. The bakufu replied by beheading the entire six-man Chinese legation and ordering preparations to defend against another attack. Chieftains in Kyushu began taking a census of

An eclectic group of courtiers, grooms, warriors, and monks work, play games, and even nap in front of a stable of well-tended horses, similar to those ridden by the elite samurai. Toddling along the surrounding walkway is a monkey *(left),* who has been brought to the stable to protect the horses by warding off evil spirits.

all the warriors and equipment available for immediate duty from each household.

One elderly warrior named Saiko sent an inventory of his rice lands and a list of the members of his household: "Saiko, aged eighty-five. Cannot walk. Nagahide, his son, aged sixty-five. Has bow and arrows and weapons. Tsurehide, aged thirty-eight. Has bow and arrows, weapons, corselet, horse. Matsujiro, aged nineteen. Has bow and arrows, arms and two followers. Takahide, aged forty. Has bow and arrows, corselet, horse and one follower." Saiko ended the list by writing, "These are at His Lordship's orders and will serve faithfully."

Along the shore of Hakata Bay, a defensive stone wall ranging anywhere from five to 15 feet high and stretching for a distance of about 25 miles began to take shape. Responsibility for the wall's

in his own hand to be placed in the tombs of his ancestors.

According to traditional sources, an army of 40,000 Koreans, Chinese, and Mongols sailed from Korea in some 900 ships. A larger force of 100,000 soldiers—some Mongols but mostly the southern Chinese that they had recently conquered—left southeastern China in 3,500 vessels. Sailing into Hakata Bay, the fleet from Korea began to put men ashore on June 23, 1281. These invaders encountered fierce opposition from samurai deployed behind their newly constructed stone wall, and Takezaki Suenaga was in the thick of the fighting.

Not content to play the role of defenders alone, the samurai staged their own counteroffensive under cover of darkness. Manning small, swift boats constructed for the purpose, they attacked the large enemy transports anchored in the bay. Pulling alongside,

"I have only one wish: for my merit to be known to the shogun."

construction, which consumed five years, fell to the landholders of Kyushu. To fairly apportion labor costs, a formula was devised whereby the landholders were to build a certain percentage of the wall based on how much land they held.

By 1280 Khubilai Khan had conquered all of southern China, and the Japanese learned he intended to turn his attention their way the following spring. He had even established a new governmental department, known as the Ministry for Conquering Japan. In the Japanese imperial capital of Kyoto, the emperor ordered prayers to be said throughout the country. At the monasteries, religious services continued day and night. People thronged to the shrines of Hachiman, the war god. The emperor also sought intervention from the spirits by writing letters

they jumped aboard and challenged the occupants to one-on-one combat. Before leaving, they set the vessels ablaze. Lacking a boat, one group of samurai swam out to a Mongol ship, boarded, beheaded the crew, and swam back to shore.

Thus outnumbered but not outfought, the Japanese warriors kept up the struggle for more than 50 days. They were particularly effective against the Korean and Chinese conscripts, who had little stomach for fighting on behalf of their Mongol overlords. Then the enemy's long-delayed main force finally arrived from China, putting ashore farther west. Remarkably, though, on the night of August 15, just when it appeared that the Japanese defenders might be overwhelmed, the winds came again as they had in 1274. For two nights, typhoon-strength gales pounded the

During Khubilai Khan's second attack on Japan, in 1281, Mongol soldiers attempt to repel a group of Japanese warriors who have stolen aboard the invaders' boat under cover of night. Though vastly outnumbered, the Japanese forces used sheer wit and determination to try to stem the Mongol invasion.

coast, uprooting trees and raising immense waves that swamped all but a few hundred of the enemy ships. The Mongol losses were catastrophic. Most of them drowned, but thousands of others were stranded ashore by the storm and then hunted down and beheaded by the samurai.

Typhoons could be expected at that time of year, but most Japanese attributed this one to a miracle. The gods had intervened, they insisted, and the typhoons of 1274 and 1281 were thereafter referred to as the *kamikaze*—"divine winds." In the aftermath of the victory, demands upon the military government for rewards were heavy. The priests who had prayed for victory claimed credit for the divine winds, and they joined thousands of samurai in asking for material recognition for their deeds. The bakufu felt obliged to give the priests preference; after all, they had much influence at the court and throughout Japan. As in the previous campaign against the Mongols, however, the military governors had little to hand out. This constituted a great hardship on the fighting

ZEN AND THE WARRIOR

The practice of Zen Buddhism gained prominence in 13th- and 14th-century Japan among the ruling members of samurai society. There were many reasons for its ascendancy, including the fact that the religion had not been adopted by the court in Kyoto. But mostly Zen appealed to the samurai because it had no prescribed rituals, emphasized self-control and self-knowledge, and taught that Enlightenment came from a person's own actions. Through meditation, discipline, and concentration one could attain satori—the flash of truth. Zen also required absolute devotion of the sort that samurai already applied to their craft. The painting at right illustrates such resolve: A student of Zen has severed his arm and offers it to Daruma, the Indian holy man who brought Zen to China, to convince the sage of his commitment to becoming his disciple.

Surprisingly, though Zen was part of the Buddhist tradition, which eschewed bloodshed, in time its priests became the masters of countless warriors. But these masters did not teach swordsmanship; they taught their pupils to rid the mind of all thought during combat. As one 17th-century sword master and student of Zen wrote: "For everything there are instructions. . . . But the man who has attained [Enlightenment] gives them up altogether. He acts freely and spontaneously. He . . . is called a man of great awareness and great action." The sword of such a warrior was thought to act on its own and to deliver not death, but justice.

men. At their own expense, they had held off the invaders, and even when most could see that their prospects for reward seemed dim, they maintained preparedness for almost 20 more years, until 1300. But Kamakura was so deluged by petitioners that the bakufu decreed that no further rewards would be granted for the two campaigns against the Mongols.

This time word of Takezaki Suenaga's bravery had reached the bakufu without a journey on his part, but to no avail. The resourceful Suenaga found another means of ensuring that his service would be recognized and remembered, however: In 1293 he commissioned a series of scrolls to depict in text and paintings his valorous deeds. The scrolls, which he presented to a Shinto shrine, celebrated not only his exploits in turning back the Mongol invaders but also his success in battling the military bureaucracy.

For the samurai, the Mongol invasions brought about important and lasting changes. First, the warriors had learned about fighting in formation, a practice that eventually spread across Japan. Second, the samurai's dissatisfaction with the bakufu had reached a point of no return, and their discontent was contagious. By the early 14th century, the Kamakura bakufu was a power in decline, and alliances were forming among its enemies in the ranks of provincial warlords and members of the Kyoto nobility, as well as in the faction-ridden imperial and ex-imperial households.

Emperor Go-Daigo had begun trying to take advantage of the bakufu's weakness as soon as he ascended the throne in 1318. Unlike most recent emperors who were mere boys when they became emperor, he was then a vigorous and ambitious man in his early 30s. A serious scholar and a stubborn autocrat, he intended to rule as well as reign. This alone was a threat to the bakufu, which had grown accustomed to running the country.

Go-Daigo also intended to remain on the throne for his lifetime rather than abdicate after a few years, as had become the custom, at the behest of the Hojo clan, who served as regents. Worse,

he planned to designate as his crown prince and successor his own son, a break in the recent tradition of alternating the throne between two contending branches within the imperial family. The alternating policy had been sanctioned by the bakufu as a way of keeping the peace, and Go-Daigo's open rejection of it put the military chieftains on guard. In 1331, when they learned from one of the emperor's most trusted advisers that he was plotting to actually overthrow them, the military government sent troops toward the capital of Kyoto.

Emperor Go-Daigo fled to a monastery atop Mount Kasagi, south of Kyoto near the city of Nara, where he evaluated his situation: He desperately wanted his throne back but lacked even the semblance of an army. All he could count on was the band of warrior-monks who were protecting him in this mountain exile and a handful of samurai on estates owned by the imperial family. What he needed was a good general—a fighting leader he could trust who had the ability to raise and command a large force of samurai.

Legend has it that the exiled emperor was pondering this problem when he dozed off and fell into a prophetic dream. In it, Go-Daigo clearly felt that he would be restored to power and, more important, the dream showed him the means. Its salient symbols were an empty chair—the emperor's—facing south, under the luxuriant branches of a magnificent tree. After he woke up, Go-Daigo worked out an interpretation. He juxtaposed the Japanese character for *tree* with the character for *south*. Together the two characters composed the word *kusunoki,* or camphor tree.

Was there a warrior with this name? the emperor asked. There was, and the man was soon summoned to Go-Daigo's refuge. Kusunoki Masashige was a warrior from Kawachi, a province located south of Kyoto, between the cities of Osaka and Nara. He was about 37 years old, the son of an obscure provincial who reportedly had taken part in raids against neighboring properties. Masashige had been schooled in a Buddhist monastery, then had followed in his father's footsteps. Known as a charismatic leader, he maintained a stronghold in a mountainous region near Kawachi's Mount Kongo and commanded a devoted band of followers. Well-disciplined and skilled fighters, they functioned more like armed guerrillas than soldiers.

Masashige evidently was not a vassal of any military overlord and owed no fealty to the military government. He may instead have overseen lands that belonged to the imperial court. In any event, he professed personal loyalty to the emperor and obediently answered Go-Daigo's call to do battle against the bakufu. But he counseled patience. Victory would not be won in a single battle, he said. He urged Go-Daigo not to be discouraged by news of setbacks. "As long as you hear that Masashige still lives," he declared, "be confident that your sacred cause will prevail!"

er branch of the imperial family, thus adhering to the policy of alternate succession.

Kusunoki Masashige, meanwhile, had launched a military rebellion marked by highly innovative tactics. His plan, as he had told the emperor, depended upon "artifice as well as military force." Soon after Go-Daigo's capture, Masashige and a small group of followers were trapped by a superior bakufu force near Mount Kongo. He decided to escape, rather than fight against such odds. As he explained to his followers: "I am not likely to begrudge my life when virtue and honor are at stake. Nevertheless [it is said that] in the face of danger the courageous man chooses to exercise caution and to devise stratagems." Following that credo, Masashige had a large hole dug, filling it with the corpses of warriors from both sides who had been killed during

"In the face of danger the courageous man chooses to exercise caution."

With that declaration Masashige launched a struggle for power that would rack Japan for half a century, pitting warlord against warlord and even emperor against emperor.

As Masashige had warned the emperor, there were early setbacks. Soon after the two met, bakufu troops attacked Mount Kasagi. Go-Daigo escaped with a few high-ranking noblemen and headed toward Masashige's stronghold near Mount Kongo. Along the way these aristocrats blundered their way into the hands of bakufu soldiers. Go-Daigo was imprisoned in Kyoto and then banished to Oki, a small volcanic island 50 miles off the west coast of Honshu. In the place of the emperor they had deposed, the military chieftains enthroned a member of the oth-

the fighting. Charcoal and firewood were piled on top. Leaving one man behind, he and several hundred samurai then disguised themselves as bakufu warriors and, breaking up into small groups, slipped through the enemy lines. When they were out of danger, the warrior they had left behind set fire to the pyre. Inspecting the remains, the bakufu troops were certain Masashige and his men had committed mass suicide.

The ruse bought time for Masashige's phantom force to wage guerrilla warfare. Operating from the mountain sanctuaries he knew so well in his home region south of Kyoto, his men harassed much larger bakufu formations in a series of hit-and-run attacks. On one occasion, he tricked several thousand troops into crossing the Yodo River and then outflanked them. His

Three samurai, dressed in elegant robes, eat rice and other foods from lacquer bowls while a woman prepares to serve them sake from a wooden ladle. Newly rich warriors eagerly sought the courtly life in Kyoto, though the old aristocracy derided the rough appearance and manners of the newcomers, whom they dubbed "sudden lords."

audacious resistance encouraged others to flock to the imperial banner being raised by the exiled emperor's son, Prince Morinaga. It also spurred the bakufu to put a handsome price on both their heads: Any samurai who killed one of them was promised a generous grant of land. Such bounties, in a time when the military government was running low on resources, reflected the bakufu's deep concern about containing the revolt.

Masashige faced his most severe test early in 1333, when three different enemy armies totaling some 100,000 warriors converged on his newest bastion. Chihaya stood high up on Mount Kongo, more than 3,000 feet above the plains. The resourceful general, who had no more than 2,000 warriors, utilized the steep terrain to slow an enemy assault. He booby-trapped the slopes with felled trees, brushwood screens thick enough to deflect enemy arrows, and pits lined with sharpened bamboo stakes. As the enemy fought to make their way through these obstacles, the defenders unleashed upon them anything they could find, from logs to large wooden vats of human waste. Week after week of unsuccessful assaults up the slope so demoralized the government troops that the bakufu sent poets from the capital to join with the soldiers in poetry sessions.

Masashige's loyalists staged a performance of their own for the enemy. They fashioned two dozen life-size dummies and dressed them in armor and equipped them with weapons. One night, they placed the dummies behind shields in front of the fortifications. Expert archers were deployed out of sight behind the dummies. At dawn the hidden archers let out a shrill chorus of bloodthirsty battle cries as if ready to attack. Believing their opponents were finally coming out into the open, bakufu warriors rose to the bait and charged up the slope. The defenders let loose a hail of arrows and retreated back into the castle. The survivors renewed their assault. Just when they reached the dummy warriors and discovered they had been fooled, new troubles descended upon them. Cascades of huge rocks loosened by the defenders above them crashed down, killing more than 300 bakufu samurai and gravely injuring more than 500, according to traditional accounts.

Through such tactics Masashige and his beleaguered garrison tied up the enemy army for 10 weeks. During this period loyalists throughout the country took heart and staged uprisings against the bakufu. And there was more good news for the loyalist cause during that spring of 1333: Emperor Go-Daigo escaped from his island exile. In the predawn darkness, he fled by fishing boat to Hoki province, where he set up temporary court on Mount Funanoe, a natural fortress.

Fearing an attempt to restore Go-Daigo to power, the bakufu sent a large force westward from Kamakura under the command of Ashikaga Takauji. Takauji was a fearless commander and the ranking member of one of the leading families of the military government. The Ashikaga could trace their lineage back to the Minamoto, who had established the bakufu in Kamakura, and also were related to the Hojo regents through numerous marriages. But Takauji was shrewd and ambitious, and like his family, he resented the domination of the Hojo clan, whom he considered to be his social inferiors.

Marching westward with his troops, Takauji made a fateful decision: He was going to switch sides. He sent a secret message to Emperor Go-Daigo requesting permission to attack the bakufu garrison in Kyoto. He also rallied thousands of other defectors from around the country by sending word of his own defection in messages written on tiny scraps of paper and concealed in the topknots of his couriers. On June 19, 1333, Takauji entered Kyoto at the head of an army more than doubled in size and sworn to support Emperor Go-Daigo. They fanned out, setting fires as they moved through the city. The incinerated buildings cast such a pall of smoke over the city, wrote one chronicler, that "it was as if the scene had been rubbed over with ink." The bakufu garrison was easily subdued.

The capture of Kyoto lifted the siege at Masashige's fortress and touched off wide-scale revolts by disaffected

This 14th-century samurai, fully armored except for his helmet and riding a fine-pedigree horse with its own elaborate fittings, has been identified by some as the shogun Ashikaga Takauji. The broken arrow in the rider's quiver and the unsheathed sword held over his shoulder suggest he is returning from the battlefield.

lords and their samurai. One such bakufu malcontent, a cousin of Takauji's named Nitta Yoshisada, similarly turned against his masters and led a hastily raised army into their bastion at Kamakura. Faced with defeat, the regent set fire to the military headquarters and escaped to a monastery with more than 200 kinsmen and loyal retainers. Rather than surrender, they committed ritual mass suicide.

Though the guerrilla fighter Kusunoki Masashige had the honor of leading the regal procession back into Kyoto to restore Go-Daigo to the throne, the man to watch was Takauji. His change in loyalties had less to do with wanting to see the emperor's throne restored than with furthering his own ambitions: He wanted to be shogun, the supreme military authority, and felt it was his due as an heir of the Minamoto clan. But the emperor bestowed that title upon his own son, Prince Morinaga, and Takauji had to be content with lesser honors.

Takauji patiently bided his time while the emperor repeated the mistakes of the old bakufu in dealing with the warriors who had supported him. The problem was not lack of land for rewards, as it had been after the Mongol invasions. Plenty of land confiscated from the defeated Hojo was available for distribution to the samurai. But most of it went to court nobles who had played no role in restoring Go-Daigo to power. The emperor failed to grasp the alienation that gripped the warrior ranks and clung to the illusion that, like Masashige, they had fought out of loyalty to him rather than for the spoils that traditionally came with victory.

As samurai discontent mounted, Takauji once again switched sides. The chain of events was set in motion in late 1334, when Prince Morinaga, who had been conspiring against the Ashikaga, was arrested and held in custody by Takauji's brother in Kamakura. Go-Daigo did not come to his son's aid, and the prince was executed the following year. In August 1335 a remnant of the old bakufu forces recaptured their old headquarters of Kamakura. Acting on his own without the emperor's approval, Takauji

led an army to Kama-
kura and killed the interlopers. Defying orders to
return to Kyoto, he ap-
pointed himself shogun
and began distributing
confiscated land to his followers. Early the next year,
he defeated loyalist troops sent to chastise him as an
"enemy of the Court" and then retaliated by marching on Kyoto, where he succeeded in temporarily
driving out the emperor. Three days later, troops led
by Masashige and other loyalist generals forced
Takauji from the capital.

More determined than ever, Takauji fled westward to the island of Kyushu. Along the way, he attracted warlords disillusioned with the emperor's
restoration of civilian rule and samurai fed up with
fighting without recompense. In May 1336 he
turned back toward the east with a huge army. He
was ready for a showdown with the loyalists.

The setting was some 50 miles southwest of
Kyoto at Hyogo, the site of present-day Kobe.
Takauji had decided to advance in two forces: His
troops would go by sea, and those of his brother by
land. The loyalist commander, Nitta Yoshisada,
needed every man he could muster, including the
veteran fighters of Kusunoki Masashige. When
the emperor ordered Masashige to join the loyal-
ist defenders at Hyogo, however, Masashige objected. He saw that
Takauji's army would badly outnumber the loyalists. He wanted
to avoid a decisive battle and retreat to his old stronghold
on Mount Kongo to gather new strength. Let Takauji take the

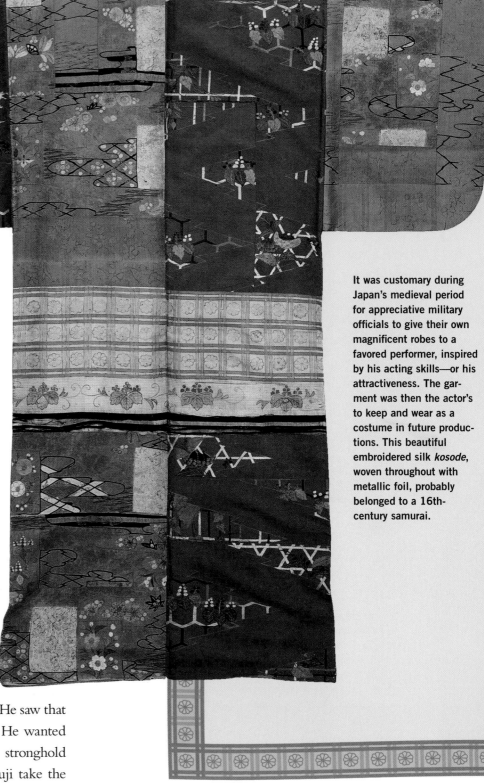

It was customary during
Japan's medieval period
for appreciative military
officials to give their own
magnificent robes to a
favored performer, inspired
by his acting skills—or his
attractiveness. The gar-
ment was then the actor's
to keep and wear as a
costume in future produc-
tions. This beautiful
embroidered silk *kosode*,
woven throughout with
metallic foil, probably
belonged to a 16th-
century samurai.

NO THEATER'S TIMELESS ARTISTRY

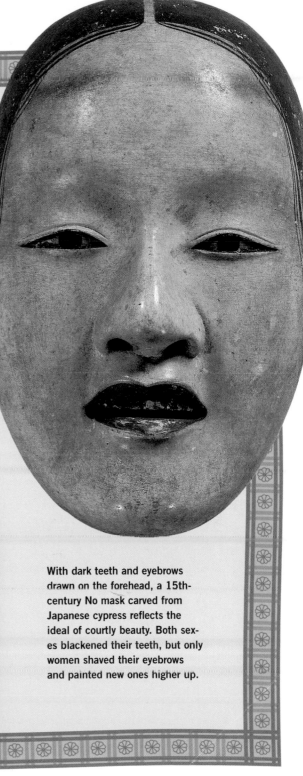

"I that am lonely, / Like a reed root-cut, / Should a stream entice me, / Would go, / I think," chants a typically anguished character in the classic 14th-century Japanese No theater drama, *Sotoba Komachi.* The highly stylized dramatic productions of No theater combined music, dance, poetry, and costume to weave tragic tales of ancient warriors, ghosts, and women possessed by the past. Evolving over time from a blend of early folk traditions and sacred dances, No achieved its classical form in the music and texts of 14th- and 15th-century playwright-actors Kan'ami and his son, Zeami. Drawn to its ritualized performances and underlying Buddhist themes, shoguns and other high-ranking military leaders patronized No theater frequently.

The No actors—all male—performed on a stage virtually devoid of props, chanting the text to the accompaniment of an onstage chorus and intermittent music provided by a flute and drums. The actors' movements were meticulously choreographed, their steps slow and measured. Some of the performers wore wooden masks, carved and painted to represent court women, warriors, and demons or spirits. By subtly lifting or lowering his head and allowing the light to cast varying shadows upon his mask, a skilled No actor could convey a range of emotions, from hatred and madness to compassion and love.

In a 17th-century screen painting, a masked No actor performs on a temporary outdoor stage set up on the imperial grounds during a special state occasion. The chorus and musicians sit against a painted gold screen.

With dark teeth and eyebrows drawn on the forehead, a 15th-century No mask carved from Japanese cypress reflects the ideal of courtly beauty. Both sexes blackened their teeth, but only women shaved their eyebrows and painted new ones higher up.

capital Kyoto, if necessary, he said. Then Masashige could strike at his lines of supply and eventually defeat him. But many courtiers advised against that course of action, and Go-Daigo, overestimating the strength of the loyalists, rejected the plan outright. Masashige dutifully led his men toward Hyogo.

According to legend, Masashige allowed his 10-year-old son Masatsura to accompany him part of the way. Before sending him back home, the warrior told his son of his conviction that he would be killed in the coming battle. Masashige gave the boy a book on military strategy and the sword he had received from the emperor. Then he said, "If you hear that I have died in battle, you will know that our country has definitely entered the age of the shogun's rule." He then made the son swear that, in that case, he would fall back upon Mount Kongo with any remaining loyalist survivors and fight for the emperor to the end.

Convinced that he is about to fight his final battle against Ashikaga Takauji, Kusunoki Masashige *(center)* pauses to say farewell to his young son, Masatsura, who bows formally before him. "I think the coming battle will decide the fate of our land, and this will be the last time for me to see your face in this life," the samurai told the boy. At his father's request, Masatsura promised to continue his family's allegiance to Emperor Go-Daigo and 12 years later met his own death while fulfilling his filial duty.

Chronicles of the time state that the Battle of Minato River, fought on July 5, 1336, pitted some 35,000 men of the Ashikaga against about half that many loyalists. The troops of Nitta Yoshisada took on Takauji's seaborne armada while Masashige's men, with their backs to the dry bed of the river, confronted the land force. Late in the afternoon, Yoshisada, thinking he was about to be attacked from the rear, suddenly withdrew from the field, leaving Masashige's troops exposed. Assailed from front and rear, Masashige fought desperately but with shrinking hope in the sweltering heat. By evening, he had lost most of his men and had sustained multiple wounds.

Rather than risk capture, he and his younger brother Masasue retreated to a nearby farmhouse. As they prepared to commit the final act of a samurai warrior, Masashige

asked his brother if he had any last wishes. "I would like to be reborn seven times into this world," said Masasue, "so I might destroy the enemies of the court." Then according to one source, they disemboweled themselves, stabbed each other, and lay down to die on the same pillow. Disembowelment, or seppuku (commonly known as hara-kiri, or belly cutting), was the customary manner of samurai suicide. An exceedingly painful death, this method was adopted by the samurai because it was thought only a person of great courage could complete it. Moreover, the abdomen was considered by the Japanese to be the physical and spiritual center of the body, although women who committed ritual suicide usually cut their throats.

Masashige's life and death fit the Japanese tradition of noble and tragic failure, and historians would honor him as one of the nation's greatest folk heroes. The victorious Takauji, on the other hand, would be cast as the villain of the era. But Takauji was not without compassion. He prayed to the Buddhist goddess of mercy, Kannon, to forgive him for his role in all the bloodshed. And after the Battle of Minato River, he made certain Masashige's head was recovered and sent to his family. He did this out of respect, he said, observing that "no doubt his widow and child would like to see him again, even in death."

Takauji reentered Kyoto in triumph and installed on the throne a 15-year-old member of the other branch of the imperial family. Two years later, the young emperor officially named the warrior to the job he had wanted and had unofficially seized, that of shogun. He was the first of 15 shoguns from the Ashikaga family, a new military dynasty that, like the deposed bakufu at Kamakura, would rule the country in the name of the emperor. Instead of maintaining stability, however, they would preside over more than 200 years of turmoil.

For over a half-century, the strife centered around the extraordinary existence of two emperors. Go-Daigo, refusing to accept his supposed replacement, had fled into the Yoshino, a mountainous district some 60 miles south of Kyoto. There, he established his own imperial court and line of succession. Japan now had two emperors—one ruled from the northern court at Kyoto, the other from the southern court at Yoshino.

Warriors and warlords supported the emperor of their choice—rarely out of ideology or loyalty but simply for personal and family gain. A notable exception was the son of the martyred hero Kusunoki Masashige. In 1347 Masatsura honored his father's last wish by taking over as commander of the southern army of the late Go-Daigo's direct heir. But a number of families had members fighting on opposite sides, sometimes deliberately, to make sure they were aligned with the victor whatever the outcome.

In the case of the Ashikaga family, internal tensions and hatreds dictated allegiances. Takauji's brother Tadayoshi went over to the southern cause, and the shogun had him murdered. After this execution, Takauji's son also defected. On four occasions southern forces actually seized the northern capital of Kyoto but were unable to hold it. Finally, in 1392, the third Ashikaga shogun managed to put an end to the southern court. He most likely tricked the southern emperor into abdicating by promising to return to the old policy of alternate succession—a promise he had no intention of keeping.

Over the years the Ashikaga shoguns became less interested in military affairs and more engaged in living and acting like court nobles. Ashikaga Yoshimasa, who headed the bakufu a little more than a century after his ancestor Takauji, epitomized this tendency. While provincial lords feuded in the countryside, Yoshimasa spent his days presiding over lavish court functions. He patronized the elaborately nuanced tea ceremony where friends with similar aesthetic interests gathered to drink tea and admire art objects displayed by the host. Under his patronage, arts such as delicate ink painting and the subtle drama called Nō flourished. But harsh taxes to pay for it all bankrupted the farmers and spurred uprisings by starving peasants. The government came to a virtual standstill because Yoshimasa allowed his wife, mother, and mistress to veto any official edict they disliked.

What finally thrust Japan into outright chaos was Yoshimasa's decision to retire after nearly three decades. He designated his brother as successor. But then his wife gave birth to a son and insisted the infant be named shogun. In 1467 the dispute set off a furious civil war. The fighting raged in and around the capital for a decade, destroying most of the city; then it spilled over into the provinces. In Kyoto, the streets were clogged with dead bodies, and cartloads of severed heads were collected as trophies. Much of the population had fled. After five months of fighting, observed a bakufu official, "the flowery capital that we thought would last forever to our surprise is to become the lair of wolves and foxes." In a short poem he lamented: "Now the city that you knew has become an empty moor, from which the evening skylark rises while your tears fall."

Thus began the 100 years of conflict known as Sengoku Jidai—the Age of the Country at War. Japan fragmented into scores of virtually autonomous domains. Each was ruled by one of the

Farmers unload bales of rice for delivery to the village headman, in payment of their yearly taxes in Japan's basic currency of rice. The headman would then pay the taxes to the proprietor. Farmers were allowed to keep only a small portion of the crops they had cultivated, an amount that grew even smaller under the harsh taxes of the Ashikaga shoguns.

powerful provincial barons known as daimyo. The daimyo made their own laws, built fortified towns to house their samurai retainers, and warred with their neighbors. Where many warriors upheld the virtues of loyalty and duty exemplified so dramatically by Kusunoki Masashige, others defied their overlords and switched sides at will like Takauji.

On November 9, 1568, a thin, sparsely bearded warlord named Oda Nobunaga entered the capital city of Kyoto at the head of a column of foot soldiers and mounted samurai. At his side rode a member of the Ashikaga family. In what had become a familiar scenario, this man, Ashikaga Yoshiaki, wanted to supplant his cousin and become the 15th member of the family to serve as shogun. Nobunaga had agreed to help him by forcing out the warlords who protected the cousin. But Nobunaga had no interest in bolstering the long-diminished power of the Ashikaga. He simply wanted to use the legitimacy of the shogun's office to further his own aspirations, which happened to be summed up in the motto engraved in his personal seal: *tenka-fubu*—"rule the empire by force."

Nobunaga was not the first of the provincial daimyo to dream of unifying their fractured nation. But at age 34 he was an innovative military tactician and a strange amalgam of aesthetic sensibility and ruthless brutality. Before battle he could perform a traditional dance and sing a delicate verse about the transience of life and then go on to massacre his enemies, even burn them alive. By seizing Kyoto, the traditional seat of the nation's imperial and political authority, he ended the Age of the Country at War and took the vital first step toward unification. He was prepared for even greater strides with the help of two top lieutenants—Toyotomi Hideyoshi, a former foot soldier of humble birth, and Tokugawa Ieyasu, a one-time enemy who would complete the work when both Nobunaga and Hideyoshi were gone.

A native of Nagoya, 75 miles east of Kyoto, Nobunaga was the son of a minor but ambitious feudal chieftain in the little province of Owari. He was so wild as a youth that a longtime retainer of the family committed suicide in hopes that this desperate act would settle him down. When his father died in 1551, Nobunaga assumed responsibility for the family's growing realm. Some members of the clan objected to his ascension. Nobunaga, who was not yet 20 years old, responded by raising a 1,000-man army that subdued the opposition; the casualties of that clash included an uncle and his younger brother. By his late 20s, the ruthless warrior controlled most of the province.

Nobunaga's aim now was to utilize his growing military skill and small army to block incursions from neighboring warlords. One of the most ambitious of these daimyo

SAMURAI WOMEN

Men were not the only samurai. Women, like their brothers, inherited samurai status, though they rarely appeared on the battlefield. An exception was Tomoe Gozen, who fought in the service of a 12th-century Minamoto leader. Battling a formidable opponent, she flung herself upon her enemy and, "grappling with him, dragged him from his horse ... and cut off his head."

Most female samurai remained behind the battle lines, where they ran the family estates. But they did receive martial-arts training utilizing the naginata, a polearm with a blade about one to two feet long. If the household was attacked, the women were prepared to meet the invaders with deadly force. Curved and sharpened on one side, the naginata's blade could slash a horse's legs or deliver a mortal blow to a warrior on foot.

Honor and loyalty were just as important to these women as to their husbands. Military leader Oda Nobunaga's sister Oichi (right), who was called "the most beautiful woman under heaven," was given in marriage twice to foster temporary peace. Her first husband was killed in an attack by her own brother when the peace dissolved. When her second husband was attacked as well, by her brother's ally Toyotomi Hideyoshi, Oichi sent her daughters to safety but refused to leave. Once defeat became certain, Oichi offered her husband the ultimate sign of love and loyalty, choosing to commit suicide with him.

was Imagawa Yoshimoto, whose domain was based in Suruga (55 miles southwest of modern-day Tokyo). Yoshimoto already was an enemy, having helped foment the dissension in Nobunaga's clan. In June 1560, Yoshimoto led 25,000 men into Nobunaga's province of Owari. Nobunaga learned the invaders were camped in the southeastern part of his province, in a narrow valley he had roamed as a boy. He led his much smaller force—perhaps 3,000 men—along a mountain trail and hid them behind a ridge. The enemy was celebrating earlier victories when a sudden rainstorm struck with powerful fury. As the sky cleared, Nobunaga's men poured down into the valley, routing the invaders and taking the head of the warlord Yoshimoto.

This battle was a pivotal point in Japanese history. Suddenly transformed into a national figure, Nobunaga began looking beyond the boundaries of his province. He made a pact with Tokugawa Ieyasu, whose base was to the east in Mikawa province. That alliance, which protected Nobunaga's eastern front, remained remarkably intact until his death. Other alliances, achieved by marrying off his daughter and younger sister, protected Nobunaga's flanks in two nearby provinces. But as he turned westward toward Kyoto, Nobunaga had to rely on naked force and the new-style army he was forging.

Fresh tactics and modern weapons were changing Nobunaga's small but potent fighting force. He made generous use of the recent development of an infantry branch, known as *ashigaru,* or lightly armored foot soldiers. Armed with long spears, they required far less training and matériel support than mounted samurai and were typically recruited from among the peasants. These foot soldiers were helping change Japanese warfare from a series of individual matches between samurai to massed clashes between armies, in the fashion of the Mongols centuries before. Nobunaga contributed to this trend by arming his ashigaru with exceptionally long lances, up to 21 feet in length, and deploying them in tight and effective formations.

Nobunaga also began equipping his foot soldiers with even more innovative weapons—firearms. The Japanese had experienced the effects of gunpowder

This gilded and lacquered receiving room is from the Ninomaru Palace, built inside Kyoto's Nijo Castle compound by Tokugawa Ieyasu's grandson Iemitsu in 1624. A mural of a wind-shaped pine tree dominates the panel against the far wall.

Wild birds perch on tree limbs amid clouds of gold and grandly plumed roosters strut on golden ground in this detail from a 17th-century folding screen *(right)*.

NATURE INDOORS

As Japan's warlords grew increasingly wealthy—surpassing even the imperial court—they turned from war to cultural pursuits. "How can a man discharge the duties of his rank and position without combining the peaceful and military arts?" asked one of Tokugawa Ieyasu's advisers in the late 16th century. Daimyo and shoguns built magnificent castles and filled them with priceless objects. They then commissioned artists to decorate the sliding doors and folding screens of their inner chambers.

Artists of the Kano school—descended from the 15th- and early-16th-century painter Kano Masanobu—obtained most of these commissions because of their skill in merging Chinese ink-painting styles with Japanese decorative methods. Using nature as a frequent motif, often within the context of the changing seasons, the Kano artists produced beautifully detailed, delicately executed murals of flora and fauna against an opulent gold-leaf background.

earlier, in the Mongol invasions of the 13th century. But guns were not introduced until 1543, when a Chinese junk arrived at Tanegashima, a little island just south of Kyushu, with three Portuguese adventurers aboard. Two of them carried matchlock muskets, which the lord of Tanegashima purchased and the Japanese quickly began to manufacture. Upstart warlords like Nobunaga, who had not yet recruited a large corps of experienced samurai, were among the early enthusiastic customers. Nobunaga found that after a few weeks of training a peasant armed with a musket could stand against the most skilled samurai swordsman.

Relying on these weapons and tactics and his own fierce determination, Nobunaga fought his way westward into Kyoto in 1568. There he held his troops under firm discipline and guaranteed the safety of the civilians, which won him the support of even the court nobles. And although he ignored the emperor and in 1573 deposed the last of the Ashikaga shoguns, whom he had used as a pawn for occupying the capital, Nobunaga was not tempted to take the shogunal title for himself. He did accept high court titles and continued to dominate the city and the dozen or so rich provinces in central Japan. But by choosing to place the interests of the general populace above those of his own family, he commanded much respect.

Nobunaga was not a religious man, but the pioneer Jesuit missionaries arriving from Portugal found the brutal warlord remarkably cordial. He openly admired their intelligence and courage, and they appreciated his support of their work, which in his lifetime would lead to the establishment of about 200 churches and the conversion of at least 150,000 Japanese to Christianity. One day in Kyoto, Father Luis Frois found Nobunaga supervising the construction of a castle, striding around in a tiger-skin cloak thrown over rough clothes. "He is rough-mannered, contemptuous of all the other kings and nobles of Japan whom he addresses brusquely over his shoulder as if they were inferiors," Frois wrote. "He openly proclaims that there are no such things

as a Creator of the Universe, nor immortality of the soul, nor any life after death."

Nobunaga favored the Jesuits because he hated the Buddhists. He considered the Buddhist sects, with their warrior-monks and leagues of militant peasants, to be among his most dangerous rivals, ranking alongside the most powerful warlords. In 1571, after the Tendai monastery, overlooking Kyoto, on Mount Hiei, gave sanctuary to some of his enemies, Nobunaga is said to have surrounded the base of the mountain with 30,000

In this screen painting, Oda Nobunaga and Tokugawa Ieyasu's musket-bearing forces *(left)* meet the charge of traditional sword-wielding warriors on the battlefield at Nagashino in 1575. The carnage wreaked by guns changed Japanese military tactics and armament.

foot summit of Mount Hiei, burning temples and shrines indiscriminately and slaying some 3,000 persons—men, women, and children who had taken refuge there, as well as the monks. Wrote one observer, "The whole mountainside was a great slaughterhouse, and the sight was one of unbearable horror."

Nobunaga was not invincible, however. Since 1570, his troops had dealt unsuccessfully with several uprisings by another Buddhist sect based south of Kyoto, near present-day Osaka. A militant form of Buddhism known as the True Pure Land sect, which imbued adherents with a deep religious fervor, had attracted a number of peasants and other poor people who were organized into an armed force. Determined to put them down once and for all, Nobunaga attacked one of the sect's monastic complexes at Nagashima in 1574. Even with the help of pirates who fired large-caliber muskets from the seaward side, it took more than a month to overwhelm three of five bastions. Then, vowing to destroy the sect "on every hill and valley," Nobunaga ordered the construction of a stockade around the remaining two strongholds. The implacable warrior had the complex set afire, roasting alive the 20,000 persons trapped inside.

The sect was subdued but not completely subjugated by this brutality. Before he could finish the job, Nobunaga was contacted in early 1575 by his former enemy and now ally in the east, Tokugawa Ieyasu. Ieyasu was under siege in his home province of Mikawa by Takeda Katsuyori, the son of one of Nobunaga's oldest eastern rivals. Nobunaga responded with a force of 38,000 men, many of them armed with muskets. In a display of tactical genius, he deployed 3,000 of his musket men behind wooden palisades designed to block the charge of the famous Takeda mounted samurai. Because it took considerable time to load a musket, Nobunaga placed his men in three ranks. He ordered them to fire on command in rotation so that two ranks would be loading while one fired. Thus, when the enemy horsemen charged in four successive waves, they were cut down by successive volleys, which

men. Two of his followers reminded him that it was one of the holiest places in the country and that for eight centuries the warrior-monks there had served as guardians of the imperial palace. But there was no stopping Nobunaga, even after the monks offered him hundreds of gold bars to lift the siege. One autumn day his men methodically worked their way to the 2,800-

came every 10 seconds and felled no fewer than 10,000 warriors.

Nobunaga was an innovator in other ways as well. In battle against a monastery fortress on the Pacific, for example, he once employed ships armed with small cannon and clad in iron armor. And when he decided to construct a castle, Nobunaga built the largest one Japan had ever seen, with its own sprawling barracks and a central fortress towering seven stories high. But he was not destined to die there in a luxurious bedchamber. In 1582, while staying in Kyoto, he was assassinated by one of his leading generals. Nobunaga did not go easily, as recounted by Father Frois:

"They found him and forthwith shot him in the side with an arrow. Pulling the arrow out, he came out, carrying a *naginata,* a weapon with a long blade made after the fashion of a scythe. He fought for some time, but after receiving a shot in the arm he retreated into his chamber and shut the door. Some say that he cut his belly, while others believe that he set fire to the palace and perished in the flames. What we do know," the Jesuit continued, is that "there did not remain even a small hair which was not reduced to dust and ashes."

Nobunaga's top lieutenant, Toyotomi Hideyoshi, immediately

avenged his leader's death and seized power. A commoner, Hideyoshi had begun as a menial in Nobunaga's army in its early days in Owari and had risen through the ranks because of his exceptional bravery and tactical skills. His engineering feats were legendary. He once had laid siege to a castle by having his men divert enough river and rainwater to threaten the enemy with inundation.

Hideyoshi possessed the military acumen of his predecessor, Nobunaga, but also understood the value of persuasion, compromise, and conciliation and used them brilliantly. To retain Nobunaga's power base in central Japan, Hideyoshi had to subdue several of their old allies. When he failed to defeat his strongest former ally, Tokugawa Ieyasu, in two major battles, he granted him virtually independent dominion over lands in the east and gave him his sister in marriage. He also allowed Ieyasu to hold his mother as hostage to allay fear that he might vio-

late their truce. By deftly alternating the carrot and the stick, Hideyoshi realized the dream of his mentor Nobunaga and gained control of all of Japan, from Kyushu in the west to the provinces in the east. Unlike Nobunaga, he did not destroy his enemies but absorbed them, allowing regional warlords to maintain their domains so long as they swore loyalty to him.

By 1590 he was the overlord of all 66 provinces. Because of his low birth he could not assume the title of shogun, but he managed to have the emperor appoint him regent by means of a clever ruse: He persuaded a descendant of the old Fujiwara family of regents to adopt him, thus qualifying him for elevated status. Hideyoshi not only ruled Japan, but he also became perhaps the wealthiest man in its history up to that time by exploiting the country's ample resources of gold and silver. He

Members of the court *(on the raised platform)* view springtime dancing and merrymaking under the cherry blossoms *(at left and right)*. During lulls in campaigns or when the strain of office became too great, the regent Toyotomi Hideyoshi often staged elaborate musical entertainments, tea ceremonies, and banquets at court.

restored the imperial palaces and built a teahouse covered completely with gold leaf.

Something of his magnanimity to his own samurai was shown in 1590 during a four-month siege at the stronghold of his last remaining rival. To ease the tedium and make the extended operation as pleasant as possible, he imported merchants displaying their wares, jugglers, musicians and other entertainers, and even prostitutes. He also ordered his warlords to summon their concubines. To his wife, he expressed his longing to see their young son and reassured her: "I have shut the enemy up in a birdcage, there is no danger, so please do not worry." Ever practical, he asked that she send his favorite concubine, Yodo, to lighten his own tedium.

Yet Hideyoshi could also be brutal and ruthless. His nephew Hidetsugu had already been named regent when one of Hideyoshi's concubines bore him a son. Suspicious that his nephew was moving against him and wanting to establish the future for his own son, Hideyoshi ordered Hidetsugu and his chief followers to commit suicide. But Hideyoshi did not stop there. As Father Frois wrote, the Japanese leader's "purpose was to destroy the women, wives, and children of all those that he had already murdered." By Hideyoshi's order, the condemned were drawn through the streets in carts, for public display, then taken to the execution site. Here Hidetsugu's "three children were first murdered, and then all the other Ladies in rank one after an other were taken out of the cart; and . . . their own heads were stricken off."

Perhaps the most surprising aspect of Hideyoshi's character was his determination to bar an ascent such as his own. For the past century or so local peasants and warriors had risen to power by overthrowing their lords. He believed that such constant upheavals threatened the country's stability and the supremacy of the military autocracy, which he now dominated. To forestall such a possibility, he issued a series of edicts aimed at freezing the feudal structure of

Breathtakingly beautiful yet formidable in its defenses, Himeji Castle perches atop a hill, gleaming in the sunlight. It is called the White Heron for the white plaster finish on its walls and because it sits like a watchful bird protecting all below it. The original structure was presented to Hideyoshi *(below)* by an ally; it was greatly enlarged by later owners.

Japanese society by keeping the classes distinct, fixed, and hereditary. Peasants were prohibited from leaving their farms and becoming warriors. Warriors in turn were ordered to remain with their current daimyo and take up residence in castle towns under the warlord's direct control.

To reinforce these policies, Hideyoshi set out in 1588 to disarm all but the samurai. In the Great Sword Hunt, everyone but warriors had to turn in their swords, bows, spears, firearms, and other weapons. Hideyoshi reassured the people that weapons "collected in the above manner will not be wasted." They would be melted down and used as nails and bolts in the construction of the enormous statue of Buddha already going up in Kyoto. "Farmers will benefit not only in this life but also in the lives to come."

Having reunified the nation and set his stamp

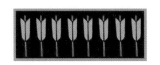

troops and was able to die peacefully at age 62 or 63 in bed at the Fushimi Palace. He left a poem—"Ah! as the dew I fall / As the dew I vanish. / Even Osaka Fortress / Is dream within a dream."—and a legacy as one of Japan's most famous heroes.

The mandate to consolidate Japan fell now to Tokugawa Ieyasu. Short, stout, powerfully built, and in his mid-50s at Hideyoshi's death, he was known to many samurai for his thunderous battle cry. Ieyasu had been Nobunaga's enemy and then a devoted ally. His relationship with Hideyoshi had been tenuous at first but then at the end so trusting that he had been made one of the official guardians of that leader's five-year-old son, Hideyori. The guardians swore they would protect the boy until he was old enough to take his father's place, but the council quickly split into factions, each claiming to be acting in the boy's interest.

"Ah! as the dew I fall
As the dew I vanish."

on Japanese society, Hideyoshi looked abroad. Perhaps infected by the same mania for conquest that had driven Khubilai Khan to twice invade Japan three centuries previously, he decided to establish military supremacy over China and Korea. In 1592 he sent an army of some 150,000 onto the Korean peninsula. Within a month, the Japanese had captured Seoul and were marching toward the Yalu River. Then Chinese forces under the Ming dynasty swept across the river and drove back the invaders. In 1597 Hideyoshi dispatched another force of more than 100,000 sword-wielding samurai and musket-equipped foot soldiers. Never before had Japanese warriors ventured abroad so aggressively.

Only the death of Hideyoshi the following year ended the fruitless slaughter in Korea. He had wisely not accompanied his

The issue was settled in 1600 in a battle northeast of Kyoto near the little village of Sekigahara. Ieyasu, leading a coalition of lords from his power base in eastern Japan, emerged the victor.

A descendant of the old Minamoto clan that had once monopolized the position of shogun, Ieyasu had the emperor appoint him to that office in 1603. He hoped to launch a dynasty and had the title bestowed on his young son two years later; however, he continued to govern as the so-called retired shogun. He moved his headquarters to the castle town of Edo (later Tokyo), among his own domains in the east.

True to Ieyasu's deathbed promise to his old ally Hideyoshi, he kept his young ward Hideyori safe in the Toyotomi family's enormous castle at Osaka. But as Hideyori approached adulthood,

Amid the clash of swords and polearms, one of Tokugawa Ieyasu's captains, wearing a horned helmet, leads an attack on the defenders of Osaka Castle. Inside this formidable keep, Hideyori, son of the great Hideyoshi, held out for weeks. In the end, he committed suicide in the tower, leaving his wife and his son to be executed.

he began attracting thousands of disgruntled samurai who had lost out under the new regime. To Ieyasu, the boy now represented a threat to the nation's new unity and to his own supremacy. In 1614 Ieyasu had his men lay furious siege to Osaka Castle, bombarding, burning, and battering their way in. Finally, in 1615, trapped in the fortress, the young man he had sworn to protect committed suicide rather than surrender.

Though Ieyasu himself died the following year, he had passed on the mantle of leadership to his son. His family's rule would endure, the city of Edo would grow to become the center of power in Japan—perhaps the largest city in the world at that time—and under the Tokugawa shoguns, the country would enjoy unity and peace for the next 250 years.

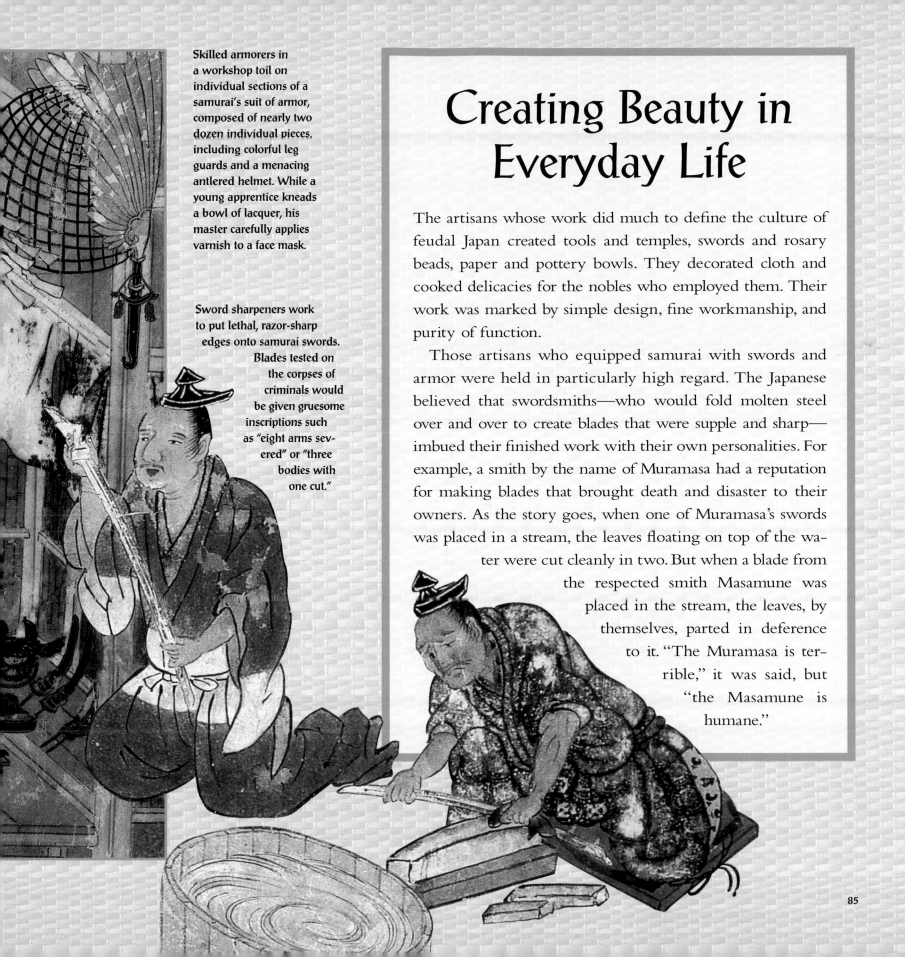

Skilled armorers in a workshop toil on individual sections of a samurai's suit of armor, composed of nearly two dozen individual pieces, including colorful leg guards and a menacing antlered helmet. While a young apprentice kneads a bowl of lacquer, his master carefully applies varnish to a face mask.

Sword sharpeners work to put lethal, razor-sharp edges onto samurai swords. Blades tested on the corpses of criminals would be given gruesome inscriptions such as "eight arms severed" or "three bodies with one cut."

Creating Beauty in Everyday Life

The artisans whose work did much to define the culture of feudal Japan created tools and temples, swords and rosary beads, paper and pottery bowls. They decorated cloth and cooked delicacies for the nobles who employed them. Their work was marked by simple design, fine workmanship, and purity of function.

Those artisans who equipped samurai with swords and armor were held in particularly high regard. The Japanese believed that swordsmiths—who would fold molten steel over and over to create blades that were supple and sharp— imbued their finished work with their own personalities. For example, a smith by the name of Muramasa had a reputation for making blades that brought death and disaster to their owners. As the story goes, when one of Muramasa's swords was placed in a stream, the leaves floating on top of the water were cut cleanly in two. But when a blade from the respected smith Masamune was placed in the stream, the leaves, by themselves, parted in deference to it. "The Muramasa is terrible," it was said, but "the Masamune is humane."

A Sacred Task

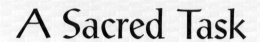

The construction of temples and shrines provided steady work for many craftsmen during the era of the samurai. Out of the bloodshed of war sprang monuments in the form of monasteries and other places of worship, which were built and supported by wealthy samurai and often dedicated to the memory of their fallen comrades. In addition, fires, earthquakes, and typhoons—and the occasional marauding band of warriors—frequently leveled various types of structures in Japan, thus creating a need for constant rebuilding.

Japan was rich with timber, making wood the favored construction material for most sacred buildings. Simple woodcutters who lived in the forest felled the trees, while skilled carpenters, directed by an overseer, peeled the bark and made the finished planks. Even though the tools they had were extremely limited—a few saws, mallets, hatchets, axes, knives, wedges, and adzes—the artisans fashioned remarkably precise and high-quality boards.

In order to put up their buildings quickly, carpenters followed the efficient Chinese method of assembly-line labor brought to Japan in the late 12th century. Some workers made only roof brackets, whereas others worked solely on floors or pillars. Every worker had a well-defined role—down to the frugal apprentices who picked up the shavings and the stray bits of wood that littered the construction site at the end of the day.

Following guidelines marked on a thick block of wood by an ink-soaked string, two sawyers cut planks with their long, two-handled saw. The man standing on the beam ensures that planks are cut to the prescribed width.

Seated under an umbrella, Haji Nobu-
oada, a political leader and clan chief,
supervises the construction of a shrine
he commissioned to honor a deceased
family member. Loggers fell trees in
the forest *(left)* while carpenters make
finished planks and lift them into place.

Wood sculptors put the finishing touches
on a Buddhist statue, designed to reside
in a village shrine or temple. Monasteries
often retained artisans or talented priests
to carve images of the deities that they
wished to honor.

Masters of the Kitchen

In most households, the women of the family prepared meals in small kitchens with earthen floors, a wooden sink, and a wood-burning cookstove. But wealthy families often employed professional cooks and kitchen helpers, who were almost always male.

Cooks served a long apprenticeship, during which they learned the secrets of a variety of fish, game, and vegetable dishes. After they had mastered the culinary arts, cooks acquired the badge of their profession—a beautifully crafted carving knife. Other necessary utensils included basketwork strainers, mortars and pestles, and containers of wood, china, or lacquer.

The lacquerware was at times produced by artisans residing in the household. The best among them fashioned serving trays and delicate chopsticks that were so valuable they were protected in special cases and were often carried along on travels, so their owners could dine elegantly anywhere.

In this busy kitchen scene, cooks seated on straw mats wield knives and chopsticks as they prepare cormorant and carp for a meal. At the stove, a cook tends a simmering game stew as another dishes up soup using a ladle made from a seashell.

Assisted in their workshop by family members, two fabric printers work on lengths of cloth, which they will hang on the wall to dry. Applying vegetable dyes with brushes, artisans skillfully painted intricate patterns onto the fabrics.

As a customer admires a display of finished rosaries, two craftsmen work in tandem to make the beads and create holes for stringing. Other fine household goods displayed in the shop include flower vases and incense burners.

Decorative Art

Through their consummate workmanship, Japanese craftsmen elevated everyday items to the level of art. The renowned 16th-century potter, calligrapher, and sword-smith Hon'ami Koetsu, for example, devoted some of his time to making wooden boxes used to hold writing implements. Far from mundane, however, the boxes were coated with gold lacquer and bore intricate designs and inlays. Koetsu also became known for his exquisite tea bowls, which he molded by hand and gave evocative names, such as Rain Cloud. Though nobles often imported elaborately decorated pot-tery from China, most Japanese preferred their countrymen's simple, rustic designs.

Aside from swords and sword guards, metalworkers turned out a wide variety of other finely crafted yet useful items, such as tools, cooking utensils, mirrors, and sewing needles. Weavers, cloth dyers, tanners, and basket weavers, as well as makers of fans and umbrellas, were in competition with one another, each of them offering beauti-fully painted or otherwise exquisitely dec-orated wares in the marketplace.

The Japanese took particular care in crafting paper, which was used for writing, covering windows, and sometimes even for clothing. Painstakingly created by hand, Japanese paper was prized for its texture and the pattern of its interwoven fibers.

CHAPTER THREE

Peace and the Floating World

Seventeenth-century Edo teems with travelers, shoppers, porters, entertainers, samurai, and priests in this view of the theater district. Throughout the century, Tokugawa shoguns enacted policies that restructured Japanese society and brought about a peace that allowed the country to flourish and reach new artistic heights.

 Dressed in the simple brown cotton coat of a priest and the woven-straw hat of a pilgrim, the poet Matsuo Basho set forth on the Tokaido road in August 1684 with great trepidation. To his back lay the booming city of Edo and his snug hut by the river, ahead lay the countryside of Japan and the small town of Ueno, his destination, some 250 miles to the southwest. The coming journey would take him from the plains around Edo, into the mountains and back down again, and across several rivers. It seemed a daunting undertaking to Basho, a small, slender middle-aged man of delicate health. Who knew what dangers he might encounter in the countryside? As he would later write, "When I left Musashi Plain and set out on my journey, it was with a vision of my bones lying exposed in a field."

Basho's fears would prove groundless—as perhaps he should have expected, having traveled to Edo from Kyoto a dozen years before. After all, Japan was no longer torn by civil war, as it had been in the 16th century. Since the early 1600s, the country had been at peace under the iron hand of the Tokugawa. With the calm had come dramatic changes, among them safer and easier travel on government-controlled highways such as the Tokaido, a well-maintained road of sand and

93

stone, banked in the middle for drainage.

Strict policing ensured security. The Tokaido, which stretched some 300 miles from Edo to Kyoto, was barricaded at certain intervals so that the shogun's guards could check for subversives, hostages, and weaponry. Almost everyone had to have a passport. Exceptions were the *bakufu*'s direct retainers; itinerant performers, who had to prove their skills at the barrier gates; and sumo wrestlers, whose bulk was ample proof of their profession. Passports were required, barrier notices pointed out, even for "persons suffering from insanity, prisoners, decapitated heads (male or female) and corpses (male or female)." Basho felt safe enough after a few days' travel to doze as he rode down the road at dawn. "Half-asleep on horseback / I

saw as if in a dream / A distant moon and a line of smoke / For the morning tea."

Maintaining the road was made easier by the ban on wheeled vehicles. But other means of transportation were allowed, like Basho's horse. There were 53 government stations along the road, with post houses whose courtyards thronged with packhorses and riding horses, hostlers, and palanquin bearers. All were for hire, for those who had money. Most people walked, as Basho often did.

Weary travelers could refresh themselves in the villages that had grown up around the stations. There were inns, restaurants, and teahouses, where rest, food, and the companionship of attractive men and women could be purchased. Some places offered local specialty items in shops selling souvenirs and medicine. Villages below the renowned Seikenji temple, on a mountain slope about 100 miles west of Edo, sold a salve made from pine resin. It was said to be good for everything from blistered feet to sore shoulders.

The Tokaido and the four other government highways were crowded. There were seasonal processions, sometimes two or three thousand strong, of daimyo and their servants and retainers, with their horses, palanquins, and heraldic banners. Common people

Amid the lush hills of the Japanese countryside, travelers ford a stream before passing through a barrier gate on the Tokaido road *(above)*. With a disciple, the poet Basho *(near right)* traveled the Tokaido and other roads, meeting fellow poets and students *(far right)*, who often gave him gifts, such as warm socks or money for sandals, when he bade them farewell.

had to kneel with their faces in the dust when the daimyo passed. A Dutch physician named Engelbert Kaempfer, exempt perhaps because of his foreign status, stood and watched. "It is a sight exceedingly curious and worthy of admiration," he wrote, "to see all the persons, who compose the numerous train of a great prince . . . marching in elegant order, keeping so profound a silence, that not the least noise is to be heard, save what must necessarily arise from the motion and the rustling of their habits, and the trampling of the horses and men." Besides these occasional wonders, there were the shogunate's messengers—pairs (in case one should meet with an accident) of swift runners working in relays from the post houses, ringing a bell to clear the way ahead. Even the daimyo stood aside for them.

Less exalted travelers included merchants whose goods might go by sea from Osaka, southwest of Kyoto, to Edo, but who journeyed by road themselves for fun. There were peddlers selling cakes, pastries, travel handbooks, straw shoes, ropes, toothpicks, twine, and ink. There were troupes of singers, dancers, and actors. And there were groups of merry pilgrims, distinctive in their straw hats, heading for Japan's great shrines. Basho stopped at one of the most renowned, the great Shinto shrine in the province of Ise. It had been sited deep in a forest in AD 690 as a storehouse for the sacred mirror of the goddess Amaterasu, ancestor of the legendary first emperor of Japan. Every 20 years, at great expense, the shrine was rebuilt and reconsecrated.

After paying his respects at Ise, the poet continued his journey, reaching Ueno in early September. He had come to this small town southeast of Kyoto to pay homage to the spirit of his mother, who had died the year before. Walking into her home, he felt the loss wash over him, observing with melancholy, "The day lilies in my mother's room had all been withered by the frost, and nothing was left of them now."

Basho had been born 40 years before in this small castle town (so called for the castle of the daimyo built there). Here Basho's father, a low-ranking samurai, had eked out a living as a calligraphy teacher. The boy was close friends with the daimyo's son, and the two youngsters were trained in poetry together. When Basho was 22, his companion died suddenly, and deeply grieved, the youth considered a monastery. Instead, he continued his scholastic work, studying Chinese and Japanese classics, the severely elegant court poetry, waka, and the more popular verse known as haikai, which was often written communally. Poets following set rules composed alternating 17- or 14-syllable verses that played off one another's themes to make a sequence.

In 1672 Basho moved to the shogun's capital of Edo. Here, always on the verge of poverty, he continued to work and study and, as his poems became known, attract disciples. By the poet's one-room hut on the Sumida River, disciples planted a basho— a banana tree that bears no fruit and has fragile, easily torn leaves. He loved the tree. "I sit underneath it and enjoy the wind and the rain that blow against it," he wrote. From the basho he took his

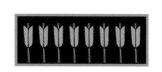

cheerful: "Shed of everything else / I still have some lice / I picked up on the road— / Crawling on my summer robes."

Knowing now that it was safe to travel about Japan, the poet did so for much of the last 10 years of his life. Because Basho made his living by teaching and composing, journeying from place to place was critical, as it allowed him to enlarge and maintain his huge circle of disciples. But he also traveled to observe the natural world and meditate upon it, seeking poetic and religious inspiration. He produced five travel books of description and poetry, culminating in the classic *The Narrow Road to the Deep North*.

In writing he transformed the often too-clever poetry of the past into 17-syllable poems of condensed and translucent images later known as haiku. His poems became an echo of the spirit he

"On a journey, ill, and over fields all withered, dreams go wandering still."

poetic name. The poet also spent a great deal of time in solitude, increasingly devoting himself to the meditative discipline of Zen. As the years passed, Basho's reputation grew, and by the time he set out on his journey in 1684, he had become a famous poet.

After honoring his mother, Basho spent many days in and around Ueno, watching the autumn and the coming winter, visiting shrines. Everywhere he went he was greeted by old friends, by disciples, by complete strangers. People asked for poems; they asked him to join them in making poems. The year turned while he was traveling—"I met on the road / The end of the year"— and the first mists of spring began. He headed back toward Edo amid blossoming flowers. His final comment on the trip was

felt pervading the natural world. He died, as he had earlier imagined, while traveling, though he took his final breath not in an open field but in a bed in Osaka, attended by a disciple. His farewell verse, written four days before his death, revealed a spirit touched forever by the road and the riches it offered:

On a journey, ill,
and over fields all withered,
dreams go wandering still.

When Matsuo Basho journeyed down its roads in the late 1600s, Japan was not only a land where travelers could pass in safety but also one of prosperity and great artistic achievement. Over the past

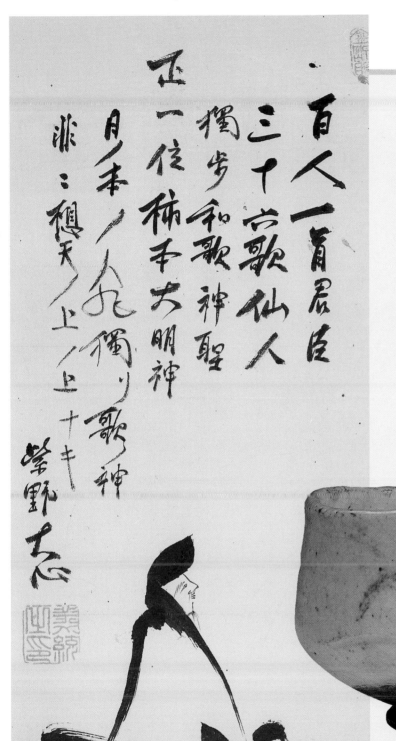

百人一首君臣
三十六歌仙人
獨步和歌神聖
正一位稀干大明神
月本ノ人名獨リ歌ノ神
非ニ想天ノ上ノ上ノ十キ

THE WAY OF TEA

Ever since 12th-century Buddhist priests returned to Japan from China with tea leaves and seeds, Japanese culture had been steeped in tea. First used by monks as a stimulant during long meditations, tea was adopted by shoguns, samurai, and merchants, who drank it at lavish parties or shared a communal bowl in a simple hut as a means of escaping the worries of the world.

The enjoyment of tea took many forms as it spread to all levels of society. In the late 16th century, Sen no Rikyu perfected a tea tradition unique to Japan. Incorporating the virtues of solitude and simplicity shared by Zen monks, Rikyu's tea ceremony was a spiritual discipline akin to meditation.

The ceremony combined the preparation and drinking of tea with poetry and art to become, as one monk phrased it, "a religion of the art of life." Following Chado (or Sado), the Way of Tea, meant taking time for tranquil reflection, such as pausing at a teahouse alcove to ponder a scroll painting like the one of the poet Hitomaro at left. Chado meant admiring natural beauty, as in the imperfections of this 16th-century handmade bowl adorned with an abstract rendering of a mountain. And Chado meant cleansing one's mind of ego and desire, as tea masters purified their utensils and served their thick, bitter green brew with modesty and reverence.

century, castle towns had grown, new towns had arisen, and cities had swelled as the population more than doubled (from some 12 million to around 30 million). A massive land reclamation had expanded paddy land by 140 percent. Mining for gold, silver, and copper had increased, as had quarrying and logging; hundreds of goods and services for daily life were also now available. This amazing transformation from the Japan of a century before was the direct result of social policies that had established and maintained peace. No longer in constant battle with each other, the daimyo and those who served them had turned their attention to agriculture and other profitable enterprises. The policies and strategies that had set it all in motion were initiated at the beginning of the century by Tokugawa Ieyasu.

Tokugawa Ieyasu was a brilliant soldier who had defeated many rivals to become shogun in 1603. Once having achieved power, however, he had to learn how to maintain it. An end to constant warfare seemed the key. He was not a scholar or philosopher, but he did have a farsighted practicality. As one chronicler put it, "Although he had conquered the country on horseback, being a man of innate intelligence and wisdom, he fully appreciated the impossibility of governing it on horseback." Gathering around him a group of talented advisers picked from among his loyal vassals, Buddhist monks, Confucian scholars, and even rich merchants, he set out to ensure that peace would prevail, and prevail under the governance of his own family.

To accomplish his goals, Ieyasu sought three things: financial strength, security, and control over Japanese society. As to the first, Ieyasu had already been daimyo of the rich eastern provinces of the plain around Edo before the Battle of Sekigahara in 1600; after his victory there, he acquired additional lands. With them, his rice revenues rose to 32 million bushels—a quarter of the total for Japan. (Further confiscations by his son and grandson eventually would bring the Tokugawa share up to half the total.) Besides land, Ieyasu confiscated gold and silver mines and assumed the monopoly on raw silk.

While improving Tokugawa financial strength, Ieyasu also sought to establish security for himself and his heirs. To ensure that the shogunate would stay within his family, he nominally retired in 1605 (without relinquishing actual power) in favor of his son, Hidetada. Hidetada's procession into imperial Kyoto for his induction ceremony at the head of 100,000 men left no one in doubt about Tokugawa strength. These formidable and loyal forces protected the shoguns, and their very existence dissuaded challenges to the Tokugawa. Further security was sought in the castle Ieyasu had begun building in

BOOKS FOR EVERYONE

With a large wooden box of books strapped to her back, a traveling bookseller markets her wares. The characters on the pack indicate that she is selling books about writing poetry. On top of the large box the seller has placed a smaller case of poetry paper, and in her hands she holds a calligraphy book and a brush. Vendors such as this one filled city streets in the late 1600s and the centuries that followed, meeting the needs of an increasingly literate public.

Publishers printed books using the woodblock method: carving pages of text onto blocks of cherry wood, brushing them with ink, then pressing them onto sheets of paper. In the latter part of the 17th century, publishers began employing professional artists to create designs that would accompany the text. Engravers carved the designs onto blocks from which a printer could run off 3,000 copies a day. Like the early-18th-century image shown here, some illustrations were hand colored. Colored pictures were also sold separately at a price roughly equal to a cup of buckwheat noodles—a snack commonly sold on the street—so almost anyone could afford to buy one.

1590 at Edo, which was located in the center of his domain, well away from the intrigues of the imperial court at Kyoto.

In constructing the castle's defenses, engineers rerouted two rivers to form a 10-mile outer moat and dug an inner moat four miles in circumference. From this inner moat rose the stone walls within which was a labyrinth of gardens, temples, and wooden palaces: an Exterior Group for the shogun's officials and guard detachments; a Middle Interior of 350 rooms for Ieyasu's private quarters; and a Great Interior of 400 rooms and corridors for his wife, concubines, and court. Between the inner and outer moats, on high ground with views of the sea, rose the palaces and gardens of Japan's daimyo.

How close a daimyo's mansion was to Ieyasu's castle was a sign of how trustworthy the ruler found him. Control of the great landowners, especially the remote and covertly hostile lords of the north and west, was critical to Tokugawa hegemony: Without it, the country would slide back into the morass of war. In the interests of security, Ieyasu divided everyone into three groups. First were the Three Houses and the Kinsmen, members of the Tokugawa clan and its cadet branches and naturally to be trusted. Next came the Fudai, or Hereditary Vassals, those who had supported Ieyasu before the Battle of Sekigahara. Last were the Tozama, or Outside Lords, those who had submitted after Sekigahara or later, after the fall of Osaka Castle in 1615. The Tozama were allowed their domains, but they were closely watched. Most Fudai held domains guarding Edo itself; others were placed so that Tozama territories were hedged in. The case was the same for the location of daimyo mansions in Edo.

On each domain, all castles but one were destroyed. From the remaining castle, a daimyo governed the surrounding land and collected and profited from its taxes. Tokugawa policies, however, reduced the daimyo's financial strength. To the central government, he had to provide military levies and labor and materials for elaborate building projects like castles, roads, and bridges. He was commanded, then legally required, to establish palaces in Edo, where he had to live in attendance on the shogun for vari-

ous periods of time. When he returned to his domain, he had to leave wives and children in the capital as hostages, in truth if not in name. The palaces, the courtly life in Edo, and the processions of thousands to and from the capital were ruinously expensive.

To codify these arrangements, Ieyasu drew up the Buke Shohatto, or Laws for Military Households, first issued in 1615, a year before his death, and revised and expanded in 1635. It established that while the daimyo ruled their fiefs, they had to obey a set body of statutes. They were forbidden to shelter fugitives from the shogunate, build new castles or repair old ones without notifying Edo, build large ships, arrange marriages without the shogun's consent, or interfere with government highways on their lands. All disputes between daimyo were to be settled by the shogunate. The government set up an inspection system to monitor compliance. Daimyo who disobeyed the laws were punished. Between 1615 and 1650, 95 lost their fiefs for infringements.

The daimyo were not the only ones the Tokugawa saw as potential threats to the shogunate and peace. Foreigners—European traders and missionaries in particular—also became a concern as the century progressed. It had not always been so. The Portuguese merchants who first landed in Japan in the mid-16th century and the Jesuit missionaries who came in their wake were welcomed—as were the Spanish with their Franciscan friars, the Jesuits' rivals. The welcome arose partly from innate courtesy and partly from the fact that they could provide an invaluable trade link for silk with China, which had closed direct trading with Japan after Japanese pirates ravaged Chinese coastal villages. Westerners also introduced firearms and other advanced technologies to Japan, useful in the 16th century's almost permanent state of war.

Tokugawa Ieyasu was as interested as his predecessors in the outside world. He got a chance to learn more of it in 1600, when a Dutch ship limped into Beppu Bay in Kyushu. This was the first time any Europeans besides the Iberians—the Portuguese and the Spanish—had reached Japan. Aboard the Dutch ship were the 24 surviving members of a five-ship expedition that had departed from Holland in June 1598.

Mounted archers await the release of a dog from the center of a double circle (above, right), ready to shoot it with padded arrows before it flees. Other archers pursue dogs that have escaped. With the peace of the 1600s and the restoration of traditional festivals, this ancient archery and equestrian training game of the samurai became a source of entertainment, as evidenced by the spectators here.

The influential Buddhist priest Ishin Suden (left) served Tokugawa shogun Ieyasu and helped him draw up 17th-century laws governing the samurai class as well as laws prohibiting Christianity.

The plan had been to sail through South America's Strait of Magellan, plunder Spanish settlements and treasure ships, then proceed to the Moluccas (islands in modern-day Indonesia) to trade for spices and other goods. From there, the ships would sail home around Africa's Cape of Good Hope. Delays, food shortages, illness, and deadly attacks by vigilant South Americans had destroyed the expedition. One ship turned back for Holland, and three others were captured by the Spanish and Portuguese. Desperate, guided more by luck than skill, the last ship made it across the Pacific to Japan. "Great was the misery we were in, having no more but nine or ten able men," wrote William Adams, a 36-year-old English pilot. "Our captain, and all the rest, looking every hour to die."

The local daimyo arranged for care and housing, but not everyone was so welcoming. Protestant Holland and Catholic Portugal were at war, and local Jesuit missionaries evidently sought to have the Dutch crucified as pirates. Fortunately for the new arrivals, Tokugawa Ieyasu received word of the situation. Though not yet shogun, he was already the primary power in Japan, and he sent a fleet of ships to bring back some of the crew. Adams, possibly the only officer well enough to travel, sailed back to Edo with Ieyasu's fleet.

JAPAN THROUGH EUROPEAN EYES

The Japanese "are very sociable . . . and much concerned with their honor, which they prize above everything else," Jesuit saint Francis Xavier wrote in the mid-1500s. His and other Europeans' notes offer a vivid, and at times contradictory, picture of Japan.

Westerners found the Japanese polite but also severe and unyielding. "A person learns rhetoric and good breeding along with the language, for nobody can know Japanese without knowing how he must address the great and the lowly," explained the Jesuit Lourenço Mexia. Yet "their Laws are very strict," another observed, "affording no other kind of punishment but either Death or Banishment."

Impressed by Japanese child rearing, 17th-century French seaman François Caron noted, "Children are carefully and tenderly brought up." A missionary, how-

ever, accused Japanese fathers of "shameless immorality" for selling their daughters as prostitutes to Portuguese traders.

Whatever the differences in opinions on other subjects, European reaction to Japanese music seemed universal. As Alessandro Valignano admitted in the late 1500s, listening to it was "a great torture for us."

As a group of Japanese approach (above, right), Jesuits welcome Portuguese merchants to the port of Nagasaki.

Using a Portuguese interpreter, Ieyasu questioned the pilot, asking, Adams wrote, "what moved us to come to his land, being far off. . . . Then he asked whether our country had wars? I answered him yea, with the Spaniards and the Portugals." The interrogation continued until midnight. Then Adams was sent off to a not-uncomfortable prison, while Ieyasu thought things over, and the Jesuits continued their demands for execution. Ieyasu cared nothing for European wars, but he did care about the possible threat to Japan from the Iberians. He had heard of their conquests of other lands and knew of the missionaries' conversions of daimyo and other Japanese and their interference in local politics.

Such interference by Jesuits in local politics had led Ieyasu's predecessor, Toyotomi Hideyoshi, to order the expulsion of missionaries in 1587 (though this was not enforced). Then in 1596, a dispute over the cargo of a Spanish galleon driven onto Japan's shores erupted between the local daimyo and Hideyoshi's representatives. During the dispute, a Spanish officer, seeking to protect his ship, claimed that the king of Spain not only would conquer Japan but used missionaries to pave the way for his troops.

Hideyoshi, who could imagine Christian daimyo calling in foreign reinforcements against him, ordered a number of crucifixions, both of Spanish Franciscans and of Japanese converts. That put an end to Spanish activity, for a while. He did not, however, suppress the Portuguese Jesuits, not wanting to jeopardize trade with the Portuguese.

Ieyasu was quick to realize that the presence of Dutch traders could relieve him of the Iberians and their subversive missionaries. Thus Ieyasu told the Jesuits, Adams learned, that the Dutch "as yet had not done to him nor to none of his land any harm or damage. . . . If our countries had wars the one with the other that was no cause that he should put us to death."

The ship's crew was released, moved to Edo, and given an allowance to live on. Adams was retained by Ieyasu to act as an adviser. He also had Adams build him a European-style ship and give him lessons in "geometry . . . and the art of mathematics." The ruler would not permit Adams to go home to his wife and daughter in England but awarded him a seaside estate 40 miles south of Edo, "like unto a lordship in England, with eighty or ninety husbandmen, that be as my slaves or servants." Apparently resigned to his fate, Adams married a Japanese woman, and they had two children.

Part of Adams's value was as an intermediary between Europeans and the shogunate. Such was his standing—and his quick learning of language and court ritual—that the Portuguese and Spanish asked him to represent them. He did, "recompensing their evil unto me with good," as he virtuously put it. He also acted as agent for the Dutch, who established a trading post on Kyushu in 1610, and for the British, who arrived in 1613.

These groups—carrying European wars of religion and territory across the seas—lost no time in attacking each other. The Spanish repeatedly requested that the Dutch be expelled—to no avail. For their part, Adams and the Dutch took care to point out that the Jesuits' converts among the shogunate's enemies were now so numerous that they could hold territory while awaiting reinforcements by sea.

Ieyasu and those around him grew more uneasy with the Iberians. Continuing reports of Iberian colonialism elsewhere in Asia and of European religious wars, the obvious strength of the huge Jesuit mission in the town of Nagasaki on Kyushu, and the fact that Ieyasu could sustain the China trade through the non-proselytizing Dutch and English all had their effect. In 1612 Ieyasu expelled the Franciscans. Two years later, he outlawed Christianity and expelled the Jesuit missionaries (a few of whom stayed behind in hiding). In 1615, when Ieyasu led his troops against Osaka Castle, it escaped no one's attention that among the castle's defenders were many waving Christian banners; the government's view of Europeans as a disruptive influence deepened. Ieyasu died the following year, and though William Adams continued to work for the shogunate after Ieyasu's death, his influence declined. He died in Japan in 1620, two decades after being cast upon its shores.

Under Ieyasu's successors, persecution of the outlawed Roman

As flames begin to burn the encircling brush wall, Spanish missionaries and their Japanese converts in Nagasaki prepare to meet death by fire while others wait to be beheaded *(foreground)* in 1622. Between 1613 and 1626, some 3,000 Japanese Christians who refused to renounce their faith were executed.

Catholics became at least as virulent as the Inquisition's punishments of heretics in Europe. Priests were expelled or executed. Japanese Christians were tortured, crucified, beheaded, and burned to death. And in 1633, Ieyasu's grandson, seeing the dangers Christian nations posed to his own, closed Japan to the world with a series of Draconian edicts. All seagoing Japanese ships were to be destroyed; no new ones were to be built. Japanese were forbidden to travel abroad; those who were caught trying or caught returning were to be executed. No foreigners were allowed in Japan except the Dutch, who were confined to a small island in the harbor at Nagasaki, and a colony of Chinese who participated in the silk trade. Except for these, Japan remained closed to the world for more than 200 years.

The Tokugawa had brought the daimyo into line and gotten rid of the disruptive influence of the foreigners. But they had not stopped there. Maintaining control of Japan, they believed, required a rigid social philosophy and class system, one that was

derived from Chinese neo-Confucian thought and gradually made hereditary and virtually unchangeable.

At the top were the samurai, the warrior class made up of the shogunate, the daimyo, and their retainers—about five percent of the population. Only they could bear the samurai's two swords—with which they could cut down offending commoners, if they wished—or bear surnames. Those who ruled at the national or local level, of course, had work to do, and they needed retainers, who usually served for a fixed rice stipend. But the abolition and reorganization of fiefs and the long peace left as many as half a million samurai out of work.

Lesser samurai were not the farmer-warriors of old: They were now forbidden to work the land. According to the Buke Shohatto, theirs were "the arts of peace and war," which "should be pursued single-mindedly." Many served the growing Tokugawa civil bureaucracy, thus combin-

On a busy street in Kyoto, two samurai argue in front of a shop selling lacquer bowls and food boxes *(above, right),* while the women in the fan shop next door go about their daily chores. Banners inscribed with the owners' crests hang in the doorways to identify the shops.

ing the skills of war and peace. Many others drifted to the cities, where they set up military schools—much in demand, because all samurai had to be schooled in the arts of war, even if there was no war. Others fell into teaching, as Basho's father had done, or renounced their class and turned to trade or to innkeeping. There still remained a quarrelsome floating population of unemployed, masterless samurai, or *ronin,* however, and they often caused problems.

In theory, the next class on the social scale was the farming peasantry. Some were well-off landowners; more were poor landholders or tenants. The lives of the latter were generally wretched: As far as the shogunate and daimyo were concerned, the farmers'

for the peasantry. "The husband must work in the fields, the wife must work at the loom. Both must do night work." They were to cut grass before cultivating the fields and make straw ropes or bags in the evenings. Tea and sake were forbidden, and as for food: "Peasants are people without sense or foresight. Therefore they must not give rice to their wives and children at harvest time, but must save food for the future." Peasants were instructed to eat millet and "other coarse food" and hoard fallen leaves for times of famine. Not surprisingly, many peasants took a dim view of this prescribed existence. There were occasional revolts. And many left the land to work in the cities as laborers or servants. Their unfortunate fellow villagers had to cultivate the abandoned plots.

After the peasants came artisans. Ordinary workers—masons and plasterers, for instance—were organized into guilds with strict apprenticeship systems. They worked for daimyo or the central government at a low wage but with an assured market. Expert artisans, especially armorers and swordsmiths, as well as such providers of luxury goods as gold- and silversmiths, artists, and clothiers, got special treatment from the shogunate and daimyo, including good pay and good housing.

Lowest of all were merchants, said to be parasites on society, creating nothing and living off the sweat of others. According to the rules of feudal hierarchy, only they could handle trade. This restriction may have stemmed from a belief that such an enterprise was unworthy of the other classes in society, but it was fortunate for Japan's merchants, for trade was increasing by leaps and bounds in the 17th century, both in the city and in the countryside. The result was that, throughout Japan, merchants—the lowest order of the Tokugawa social system—thrived.

For centuries, adventurous peddlers had been hiking rural Japan, buying and selling wares like cloth, salt, and medicine that could be toted on poles. Now traveling was safer, and the peddlers could venture farther afield. As their capital accumulated,

job was to provide tax rice. The official policy was to determine the minimum amount a peasant could live on and take the rest as tax: "These people are too comfortable," said a shogun's chief counselor in 1640, when he observed peasants on his estates living in snug houses instead of hovels. "They must be more heavily taxed." The peasants were also called upon to provide labor and horses for public projects.

As for their daily lives, injunctions posted in all villages in 1642 and 1649 stated clearly what the government had in mind

In this late-17th-century scroll painting, a group of men and women enjoy music and good food on an outing beneath the cherry blossoms. The two food-filled drawers lying on the center mat are from a picnic box like the black-lacquered one at far right, a beautiful piece decorated with gold and silver powders and inlaid shell. Increased demand for such luxury items drew growing numbers of merchants to Japan's cities.

they set up village stores and then chains of stores. Eventually they began to invest in rural land and industry.

Most merchants, however, gravitated to the castle towns and major cities, where large populations of aristocrats, bureaucrats, and warriors needed building materials, provisions, furnishings, clothing, and luxuries. Merchants handled these and other items with networks of markets and suppliers. What the merchants supplied varied greatly depending on locale, particularly in the three major cities of Osaka, Kyoto, and Edo.

Osaka, almost totally devoted to trade, had a long tradition of intelligent, conservative businessmen. Here the wholesalers were concentrated. Tending to specialize by product or region, they owned vast warehouses for the storage of tax rice, cotton, iron, paper, pottery, tea, and other goods, which they shipped around the country. Here also were bankers and moneylenders: Samurai and daimyo needed brokers to convert their rice income into gold and silver. In addition, the expensive lifestyle of the warrior aristocracy ensured the necessity of loans. Osaka was home to the chief exchange brokers, who determined the rate of changing the government-issued silver used in Osaka for gold used in Edo, as well as rates for the domains' paper money. The city's prices were the reference point for prices around the country, and its merchants were the models for others of their kind.

Kyoto, seat of the imperial court, was the aristocratic city, renowned for its style and its ancient arts, including weaving, dyeing, embroidery, and pottery. Merchants here were fewer and not as rich as in Osaka, but Kyoto had enormous cultural cachet. Trading firms in other cities liked to have branches here for the prestige.

Edo, a newer city than the others, was a fast-growing, free-spending boom town. It housed the shogunate and a huge population of samurai and was crowded with retail merchants who catered to the daimyo. Frequent fires, the most devastating in 1657, generated large building fortunes and a number of scandals here, as enterprising builders exploited government contracts. People who wanted quick riches headed for Edo.

Whatever their differences in style,

merchant families shared certain feudal attitudes: They were well aware of their position in society, and they had their own culture. They lived and worked in wards, or *cho,* designated especially for them, usually according to their trade. Each ward consisted of buildings grouped around courtyards with a community toilet, well, and rubbish pit. The buildings faced outward to streets that separated the wards, presenting to passersby their latticed facades hung with *noren,* the dark blue banners marked with the merchants' insignia.

The businesses were family affairs; the term used for an enterprise, "the house," meant both the business and the family that owned it. The first loyalty of every family member (and employee) was to the house and its ancestors. Maximizing profits honored them. Yet the welfare of the house took precedence over bloodlines. Leadership of family and house theoretically passed from father to eldest son; sometimes branch houses were set up for younger sons. If there were no sons, or if the sons were deemed not capable, merchants adopted sons to succeed them.

Sometimes these adopted sons came from among the employees, who typically began apprenticeships with a firm at the age of 12 or 13. Apprentices ran errands and received schooling; if they were satisfactory, they were considered adults and

promoted to clerkship at the age of 17 or 18 and began receiving salaries. With success, they could rise through various clerical ranks to become head clerks around the age of 30. Then an employee's salary rose; he was allowed to have his own home and to commute to work, and he could do some business on the side. If he did well enough, he might even set up a separate house. If he did, his loyalty and homage to his old house must remain unswerving.

This conservative system, with its deep loyalties and carefully documented rules, produced some remarkably long-lived and prosperous firms. Mitsui was one of the most famous. It began with the son of a samurai who had distant connections to the Echigo province. After the Battle of Sekigahara in 1600, he realized, as the family history put it, that "a settled and strongly centralized government would be more propitious to commerce than to warfare." He abandoned his rank and set himself up as a brewer and seller of sake at a town in the province of Ise. He called his shop Echigoya in honor of his father.

READING, WRITING, PLAYING

As part of learning a trade, boys from merchant families were schooled in reading, writing, and arithmetic. Many girls learned those skills as well. Though they usually did not become merchants themselves, women might deal with customers or clients and handle correspondence and accounts. More daughters of merchants attended school than did those of any other class.

But there was time for play as well. The scroll above shows parents buying dolls for their children from a dollmaker's shop in Edo. In spring, girls celebrated the doll festival, in which dolls representing the imperial family were displayed in the home's tokonoma, or ceremonial room. At summer festivals, families displayed miniature armor and weapons, and boys celebrated by fighting mock battles. Japanese children also enjoyed tops, kites, yo-yos, shuttlecocks, balls, and stilts.

This first Mitsui merchant died young, leaving his wife, Shuho, to take care of the business. Shuho did much to make Mitsui a first-rate merchant house, focusing on pawnbroking, sake brewing, and miso production. When Tokugawa Ieyasu invited provincial traders to Edo, Shuho's eldest son set up shop there; her youngest, Hachirobei, apprenticed with him. Eventually, Hachirobei used his savings to become a moneylender, and when he had enough capital, he set up as a dry-goods merchant in Kyoto with a branch shop in Edo, where he sold brocades.

Hachirobei was an innovator. It was the custom in Edo for fabric sellers to take samples of cloth, always sold in standard lengths, to the palaces of samurai customers. They usually sold on credit—an easy way to lose money. Hachirobei's Echigoya shop sold to the passing trade, under a sign that read "Cash payments and a fixed price." He also sold varying lengths to customers as they needed. This innovative approach was a wild success. Customers flocked to Mitsui, which added shop after shop until the street became one of the sights of Edo.

Besides trade, Hachirobei invested in banking operations in Edo, Kyoto, and Osaka. He did well, and the bank became an agent for the shogunate as well as a source of investment capital. Yet he would leave a will commanding his descendants not to lend money to feudal chiefs. Too many houses were ruined by nonpayments and cancellations of debt.

Before Hachirobei died, he formed his many children into 11 collateral families, or houses, whose duties to the central house and to one another were spelled out in his will. This will became the model for a family constitution, or house code, that served as a model for other merchant houses.

Such codes demanded that branch families deal kindly with one another; that they be thrifty; that they make no major decisions, such as "marriage, incurring debts, or underwriting others' debts," without the advice of a family council; and that they not retire early. A house code covered income distribution, audits, talent searches, and commercial education. ("Make your sons begin with the mean tasks of the apprentice, and when they have learned the secrets of the business, let them take a post in the branch houses to practice their knowledge," as the Mitsui code put it.) The family council was responsible for dealing with renegade members. All were to worship the gods, revere the emperor, and do their duty.

Codes like this, and the tradition of unswerving loyalty and hard work, made for prosperity and, in some cases, enormous riches. The Yodoya family of Osaka, for instance, owned 540 houses and 250 farms and counted among their possessions 21 solid gold hens with chicks; 14 solid gold macaws; 15 solid gold sparrows; 96

crystal sliding doors; a solid gold checkerboard; 17,000 rolls of velvet, silk, and brocade; and 173 rubies.

Possessions such as these put the property of even great daimyo in the shade and irritated the authorities, as did merchants who built ostentatious mansions and adorned their wives with extravagant clothing. Japan was a strictly ordered feudal society, and the symbols of that order were visually displayed—in houses, in dress, in modes of transport, in entertaining. From the government's point of view, people who decked themselves out in greater finery than their class permitted were considered guilty of challenging the system.

As the Buke Shohatto stated, "There should be no confusion in the types of clothing of superiors and inferiors. There should be distinctions between lord and vassal, between superior and inferior." The shogunate repeatedly issued sumptuary laws regulating dress. Even the puppet theaters came in for attention: "The costumes of puppets must not be expensive. Gold and silver leaf should not be used on anything. Only puppet generals may wear gold and silver hats."

These laws were repeatedly flouted. Finally, the government simply acknowledged the fact: "Embroidery has been prohibited in women's clothing. Its use has become common, however, and hereafter embroidered robes may be bought and sold if they are not especially sumptuous."

The truth was that except in rare instances—the Yodoya family's wealth was confiscated as an example to others, although the fact that daimyo were heavily in debt to them may have played a part in the decision—few were punished for display. The authorities, firmly in charge, simply registered their dislike of presumption through their laws.

For it was a gilded age, an urban culture fueled by the wealthy merchants of the late 17th century. They spent their money not only on beautiful clothes, rich possessions, and fine houses but on the arts as well. They patronized writers, artists,

Attired in kosodes that have been dyed a rainbow of colors and decorated with a wide array of geometric patterns and nature motifs, a group of 17th-century courtesans enjoy some leisure time, reading love letters and listening to music.

THE HEIGHT OF FASHION

Fashions have changed from those of the past and have become increasingly ostentatious," wrote author Saikaku in his 1688 collection of short stories on the rise of Japan's merchant class. Wealthy men and women, elegantly attired in the latest styles made from luxurious silks, satins, and brocades, could be found throughout Japan's thriving 17th-century cities.

Both men and women wore the *kosode* (or small-sleeved garment), an early type of kimono, with an obi, or sash, around the waist. Originally the kosode was a simple garment worn as outerwear by commoners and under layers of robes by Heian nobility. By the 14th century, a longer and more decorative version had become fashionable outerwear for the upper classes. Over time, both sleeves and hem lengthened, and the sash widened.

The 17th-century kosode was extremely comfortable and versatile. Tucking the hem into the obi allowed the wearer to walk easily along city streets. For formal occasions, one could don a more decorative kosode over an everyday one for a cloaklike effect.

Rich merchants and daimyo lavished money for new clothes on their wives, concubines, and daughters, who tried to outdo each other at social events. Styles for women changed rapidly as Japan's sophisticated textile industry continually offered new designs in dazzling new hues. Using the kosode as a canvas, artisans painted the material with beautifully detailed decorations—seasonal landscapes, birds in flight, delicate blossoms, seashells, or fans over striped, zigzag, or geometric patterns. Weavers created different textures by adding gold thread, embroidery, metallic foil, and appliqué.

With their powdered faces and elaborate hair styles, kabuki actors and courtesans of the pleasure quarters served as fashion trendsetters. They were often used as models in popular illustrated clothing-pattern books, like *Kosode Full-Length Mirror,* which featured "patterns and colors for your delight." Woodblock prints depicted alluring courtesans in the latest styles, as well as plumper, older women in more conservative attire.

Courtesans wearing robes decorated with narcissus and banana leaves prepare for the evening. One woman shaves her friend's hairline, as was the fashion, while another bends over a bowl, painting a dot of red saffron paste on the center of her lips to make her mouth appear smaller.

and actors and indulged in a life of the senses. In the process they created a vibrant culture of pleasure tinged with overtones of sadness. It was called *ukiyo,* "the floating world."

Opulence pervaded urban Japan as the 17th century waned. Even the shogunate spent wildly. Though Tokugawa Ieyasu had presented himself as a frugal, disciplined soldier, his great-grandson Tsunayoshi, who ruled from 1680 to 1709 in a period known as the Genroku era, lived in breathtaking grandeur and with absolute power.

Tsunayoshi's mother, Otama, was a grocer's daughter who became a concubine of the third shogun. (This perfectly honorable position was a favorite means of advancement for merchant families.) When the shogun died and Tsunayoshi's elder brother succeeded, Otama became a lay nun and devoted herself to raising her son, an intelligent child whose youth was spent in Confucian study.

In 1680, when he was 34, Tsunayoshi succeeded in his turn. He took control swiftly and severely with a much admired settlement of a complex domain dispute. It was an announcement that he intended to keep close watch on the daimyo, a pronouncement borne out in the years to follow: For various infringements during his reign he deprived more than 33 daimyo of their lands.

He kept close watch on public life as well. Edo, for instance, was plagued by gangs of ronin and overprivileged commoners. He had them rounded up. Some were executed, while others were banished, and the problems stopped. Besides this, he sponsored educational programs in his favorite Confucian studies, various other kinds of scholarship, and the arts. There were a number of compassionate innovations, as encouraged by Confu-

In a scroll painting from the 1700s, a courtesan touches up her elegant chignon, checking her work in a mirror. Like kosode designs, women's hair styles changed over the centuries, varying from extremely long and unbound to elaborate upswept hairdos, held in place by combs and pins.

cian and Buddhist practices, including care for prisoners, shelters for the homeless, protection of servants, and the prohibition of infanticide.

But some of the shogun's changes were considered proof of derangement. Believed to be influenced by his Buddhist mother, he extended his compassion to all living creatures. Among his laws were an interdiction against falconry and the sale of birds or fish as pets as well as the curtailment of hunting and fishing. Most notorious, though, were the dog laws he began to issue in 1685. These required that stray dogs be fed by townsmen, sick dogs be given medical care, and all canines be addressed by honorifics—"Mr. Dog" or "Mrs. Dog." As the laws tightened, commoners were crucified or beheaded for wounding dogs; one samurai was forced to commit seppuku, and others were exiled.

Edo, of course, was soon overrun with stray dogs. Eventually the city established compounds for them, said to hold 50,000 animals. They were fed on rice and dried fish, paid for by taxes on the citizenry. Privately, some Edo citizens took to calling the shogun and his two favorite counselors—all born in the zodiacal year of the dog—"The Three Dogs."

The shogun's position also allowed him a freedom that his Confucian principles did nothing to control. There were his love affairs, for instance: "The ruler liked sex with males," a chronicler wrote. "From among the sons of tozama daimyo and hatamoto [the shogun's retainers] down to soldiers and housemen, no matter how humble, if they were handsome, he appointed them as attendants." Homosexuality was neither unusual nor illegal, and it was not his choice of sexual companions with which people found fault. As with the dog laws, it was the extremes of his behavior.

Three puppets keep an audience enthralled during a performance at a bunraku, or puppet theater, in Kyoto. Playwright Chikamatsu Monzaemon preferred bunraku because its chanters, who told the story while the puppets acted it out, respected the author's text, while live actors sometimes improvised.

The shogun's lavish spending on his favorites, his promotion of them to the highest ranks, and his forcing daimyo to serve with them as pages caused the people to consider his actions scandalous.

Not that the citizens were prepared to protest or even comment openly. For one thing, respect for rank was strong. For another, criticism was dangerous: An artist who gently satirized the shogun in a picture book was exiled to a remote island, where he stayed for some 11 years, until Tsunayoshi died. He was thought lucky. Besides, people were occupied with their own affairs.

After all, urban Japan at the end of the 17th century was in the midst of an unprecedented cultural flowering. It was influenced by the courtly ideals and art forms issuing from Kyoto and by a kind of ideal of the cultivated gentleman, knowledgeable about all arts, that was accepted by samurai and commoners alike. But this was also a bourgeois flowering: art created by and for city people out to enjoy life.

It centered on the pleasure quarters—the city wards where prostitution and theater were licensed—in the three great cities: Yoshiwara in Edo, Shinmachi in Osaka, and Shimabara in Kyoto. Here, rules of rank were set aside and money ruled: As a novelist put it, "A guest's a guest, whether he's a samurai or a townsman."

In these districts, every sort of amusement was available. There were teahouses and restaurants; large and small theaters; sideshows with freaks, performing monkeys, and dancing dogs; street entertainers reciting folk tales or military epics; and sumo wrestlers.

The most important inhabitants, though, were women, sold to brothels as children. They were elaborately ranked. At the bottom, of course, were common prostitutes, who were displayed behind lattices to customers outside and known as *mise-joro,* or "shown prostitutes." At the top were the *age-joro,* apprenticed in childhood to older courtesans for training in music, dance, conversation, and the arts of pleasing. The aristocrats among them were classified as Pines, Plum-Blossoms, and Maple Leaves, followed by Tides, Reflections, and Moons, all titles with literary associations. They were dressed with the greatest taste and at the greatest expense and were attended by special retainers and maids. Men whose offers they accepted paid the equivalent of hundreds of dollars a night; men who kept them exclusively paid in the thousands, and a man who wished to liberate a courtesan from her house had to pay the equivalent of a handsome living wage.

People flocked to the pleasure quarters, whose chic, freedom, and gaiety provided welcome relief from the rigidities of social life. (Many kept their faces hidden, however: The quarters were off limits to samurai, and Tsunayoshi's secret police were everywhere.) The streets sparkled: "The early winter's evening at Sonezaki-Shinchi glimmered, softly illumined by the inscribed lanterns of the teahouses," the playwright Chikamatsu wrote of a street in Osaka. "Through the thronged streets young rakes were strolling, singing folk-songs as they went, reciting fragments of puppet dramas, or imitating famous actors at their dialogues. From the upper rooms of many a teahouse floated the gay plucking of a samisen."

They were pleasure seekers, but ones who also felt sadness at the fugitive nature of earthly pleasure. Theirs was the autumnal, elegiac tone long characteristic of Japanese art. Its new name, according to the writer Asai Ryoi, came from the Buddhist term *ukiyo*—the melancholy and impermanent "floating world" of transient beauty. Its adherents, he wrote in 1661, were devoted to

born to a merchant family in Osaka. Realizing that townspeople wanted to see themselves reflected and wanted excitement as well, he devoted his attention to city life. Many of his books, such as his first, *The Life of a Man Who Lived for Love*, were erotica. (The plot involves the sexual episodes of a townsman Don Juan, beginning when he is eight and lasting until, having exhausted the possibilities of Japan, he sails off to a legendary island of women.) There were also books about those who earned their livings in the pleasure quarter, books about samurai, and books about people making or losing money. Saikaku wished to show the bourgeoisie to itself, with its peculiar virtues and failings.

The townspeople's greatest pleasure, however, was derived from the livelier forms of theater that they developed and perfected. These were *joruri*—also known as bunraku, or puppet theater—and

"Like a gourd floating along with the river current: this is what we call the floating world."

"drinking wine, diverting ourselves in just floating, floating; caring not a whit for the pauperism staring us in the face, refusing to be disheartened, like a gourd floating along with the river current: this is what we call the *floating world.*"

That world became the focus of painters, printmakers, and prose writers. Spreading literacy and woodblock printing, which permitted the combination of text and images, immortalized life in the pleasure quarters in pamphlets, poems, plays, tales, and novels. Ghost stories, romances, travel guides, and critiques of courtesans were issued by the hundreds of city printers for the thousands of city readers.

The popular works were called *ukiyo-zoshi,* "books of the floating world." Their most famous creator was Ihara Saikaku,

kabuki. Both began early in the 17th century in Kyoto.

The puppet theater was the older of the two: Puppets were sometimes used to perform No plays in the 15th century, and the art developed steadily toward the exquisite refinements of bunraku, whose puppets, about three feet tall and manipulated by black-clad puppeteers, acted with startling grace and realism. Their performances were essentially tales told by a chanter to the accompaniment of the piercing notes of the samisen: The chanter narrated the story, assumed voices for all the roles, explained behavior, and sometimes sang songs or poems to create atmosphere, while the puppets mimed the parts. The beautiful dolls became, as one critic put it, "words incarnate."

Kabuki, on the other hand, began as popular song and dance,

Wearing a large straw hat to conceal his identity, a samurai chats with one of the women on display at a brothel. Lower-grade prostitutes would sit in these open reception rooms, playing music and advertising the delights within.

disreputable from its beginnings because of its association with prostitutes and actors—outcasts in the Tokugawa scheme of things. Credit for its origin traditionally goes to a woman named Okuni, sometimes said to be a Shinto priestess, who first appeared with her troupe in Kyoto in 1603. The word *kabuki* means something like "slanted," implying eccentric behavior, and Okuni's performances certainly were that. Among her costumes was a man's crimson silk robe accessorized with a golden sword, dagger, and fashionably exotic Christian crucifix.

Okuni's revues—songs and lively folk dances with rudimentary plots—drew huge crowds, not least because they were a come-on for the troupe's offstage sexual services. Kabuki performances immediately spread through the pleasure quarters. Then, in 1629,

fights in the audience over the women induced the government to ban actresses from the stage. They were replaced by handsome youths known as *wakashu,* whose erotic talents also were available, also caused public quarreling, and also were banned, in 1652. Deprived of available women and boys, the theater managers turned to more dramatic plots and stories, borrowed from No and from the puppet theater, to lure spectators. Kabuki was on its way to becoming a highly developed and stylized art form.

Both puppets and live actors drew huge crowds in the towns, if for no other reason than the sheer spectacle. The theaters offered fabulous costumes and—unlike the austere No stages—sets. A play might open with a realistic scene of a castle and a shrine, for instance, with rows of evergreens receding into the background; this would change to a scene of a palace room with painted screens; and this to fields of wildflowers and a distant view of Mount Fuji. All of it would be exquisitely, theatrically realistic, which was what the audience wanted: If the story involved the ocean, they wanted to see it; if a snowstorm was called for, they wanted snow—and bunraku and kabuki provided it

Actors, including onnagata (female impersonators), meet with wealthy patrons in a luxurious teahouse located near a kabuki theater. The female impersonators often offered their services as prostitutes; one relaxes here in a net-covered bedchamber with a client *(above, left).* Onnagata, like the one portrayed at right, were expected to live as women even outside the theater—to sustain the illusion.

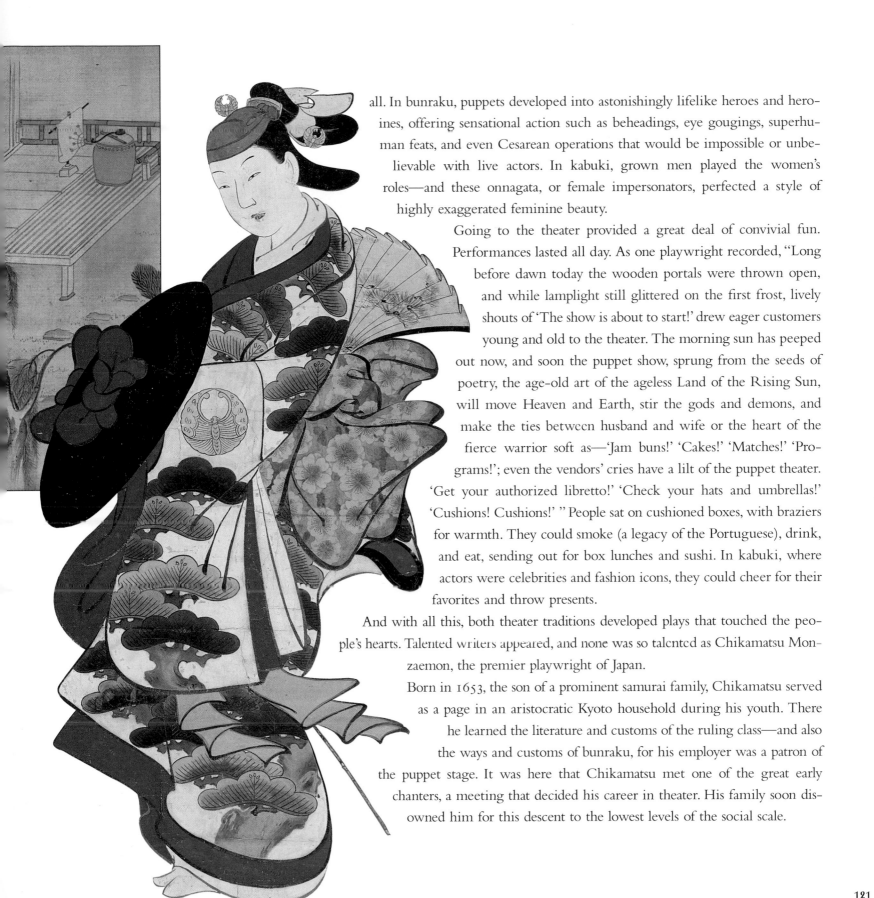

all. In bunraku, puppets developed into astonishingly lifelike heroes and heroines, offering sensational action such as beheadings, eye gougings, superhuman feats, and even Cesarean operations that would be impossible or unbelievable with live actors. In kabuki, grown men played the women's roles—and these onnagata, or female impersonators, perfected a style of highly exaggerated feminine beauty.

Going to the theater provided a great deal of convivial fun. Performances lasted all day. As one playwright recorded, "Long before dawn today the wooden portals were thrown open, and while lamplight still glittered on the first frost, lively shouts of 'The show is about to start!' drew eager customers young and old to the theater. The morning sun has peeped out now, and soon the puppet show, sprung from the seeds of poetry, the age-old art of the ageless Land of the Rising Sun, will move Heaven and Earth, stir the gods and demons, and make the ties between husband and wife or the heart of the fierce warrior soft as—'Jam buns!' 'Cakes!' 'Matches!' 'Programs!'; even the vendors' cries have a lilt of the puppet theater. 'Get your authorized libretto!' 'Check your hats and umbrellas!' 'Cushions! Cushions!' " People sat on cushioned boxes, with braziers for warmth. They could smoke (a legacy of the Portuguese), drink, and eat, sending out for box lunches and sushi. In kabuki, where actors were celebrities and fashion icons, they could cheer for their favorites and throw presents.

And with all this, both theater traditions developed plays that touched the people's hearts. Talented writers appeared, and none was so talented as Chikamatsu Monzaemon, the premier playwright of Japan.

Born in 1653, the son of a prominent samurai family, Chikamatsu served as a page in an aristocratic Kyoto household during his youth. There he learned the literature and customs of the ruling class—and also the ways and customs of bunraku, for his employer was a patron of the puppet stage. It was here that Chikamatsu met one of the great early chanters, a meeting that decided his career in theater. His family soon disowned him for this descent to the lowest levels of the social scale.

He wrote for both the kabuki and bunraku theaters, and he was largely responsible for the fine development of their two primary genres. His history plays, or *jidaimono,* were about love, honor, and revenge in noble samurai houses; sometimes they used current events in their plots, disguising the events with false names and historical settings to evade the shogunate censors. One such play, a perennial crowd pleaser, was later revised and called *Chushingura;* it is known to the West as *The Forty-Seven Ronin.* Its inspiration was an event of 1703, in which a daimyo unfairly forced to commit seppuku was avenged by his loyal retainers.

This play, like all history plays, offered the fantastic heroics and melodrama expected of jidaimono. But Chikamatsu also included scenes from the pleasure quarter, and his emphasis, as in most of his plays, was on an emotional conflict familiar to his audience: the battle between *giri,* or obligation to one's family, class, or society, and *ninjo,* or human emotions.

Such conflicts were at the heart of Chikamatsu's domestic plays, or *sewamono.* These dramas were something new and enormously popular with audiences: Their characters were not great families, past or present, but merchants, clerks, and humbler courtesans. People called the plays "living newspapers": Chikamatsu took real events and transformed them into art.

His first bunraku play in this vein—the predecessor of a number of plays on similar subjects—was based on an incident he had heard about in Osaka. It was called *The Love Suicides of Sonezaki.* In it, a shop assistant named Tokubei, having fallen deeply in love with a prostitute named Ohatsu, refuses to marry a girl his uncle has chosen for him. He must therefore return the girl's dowry. But

Backstage at a kabuki theater, assistants help actors adjust their costumes *(top and far right).* Below the screen, other actors relax to the music of a samisen; the onnagata at left knocks tobacco ash from the pipe he has been smoking. With performances starting early and continuing all day, life at the theater bustled.

a friend has tricked him out of it so cleverly that blame for its loss must fall on Tokubei. In despair at a hopeless and disgraced future, he and Ohatsu commit suicide, secure in the Buddhist hope of perfect union in another life.

The play was a raging success and was followed by others on the same theme, which were also successful. In fact, they started a vogue for real-life love suicides, which eventually inspired the censors to prohibit the word for "love suicide" in any play's title.

The exploration of the themes of love and duty, the frank acknowledgment of the powers of money, and the humble characters and their language were what made the plays so vivid and artistic and so popular. Chikamatsu turned his attention to humble, flawed people:

Tokubei is a weakling and a fool; Ohatsu is not a high-ranking courtesan but a common prostitute, although one with a heart of gold. He endowed his characters with perfect, unflinching love, expressed in the most ravishing poetry, and so raised them to the levels of the heroes and heroines of the history plays.

Audiences, who after all might have known people just like them, were moved and enchanted. Their hopes and fears, their grief at the fleeting pleasures of the world, were given universal meaning in passages such as the one Chikamatsu wrote for his lovers as they made their journey toward death:

Farewell to this world, and to the night farewell.
We who walk the road to death, to what should we be likened?
To the frost by the road that leads to the graveyard,
Vanishing with each step we take ahead:
How sad is this dream of a dream!

Chikamatsu's words seemed to capture the *fin-de-siècle* spirit of the age. Genroku, the era of Basho and Saikaku, of Chikamatsu and of countless artists, drew to its close. It died in a burst of natural disasters. Edo suffered a terrible earthquake and fire in 1703; 37,000 died. In 1707 Mount Fuji erupted, covering the surrounding provinces with layers of ash: The sky over Edo was black for two weeks.

The following year brought floods, fires in Kyoto that leveled the emperor's palace, a typhoon that destroyed crops around Osaka and Kyoto, and a great fire in Osaka. A measles epidemic killed thousands.

Among them was the shogun Tsunayoshi, who died in 1709. It was as if, some said, the shogun's extravagance and mismanagement had brought a plague of disasters to his nation. And after his death, the great social and cultural flowering of Tokugawa Japan settled into a long autumn of decline.

禅

Zen Gardens

Mushin, or "no-mind-ness," is the unselfconscious state sought by Zen practitioners. Novices might learn it from a master, who would pose word puzzles known as koans to free the mind from rational thought, or they could turn to nature. In hillside study huts and temples like the one at left, monks contemplated nature's mysteries and virtues. Enlightenment could take years of meditation—watching trees change and rocks endure—or it could come suddenly, with the splashing sound of a waterfall or a frog leaping into a pond.

Monks designed landscapes to serve as visual koans: verdant gardens with intimate paths winding to teahouses, and dry gardens of sand and stone. Gardenmaking, like poetry and archery, was an art and a spiritual discipline, embodying abstraction and austerity. Some gardeners planted only moss, others nothing at all; most avoided the sensual distractions of flowers. Like Zen priests, Zen gardens ask questions without answers. Viewers are left to find their own truths and to cast off superficial distinctions such as "living" and "nonliving." As seen in the gardens that follow, water speaks without words, hedgerows undulate without motion, rocks eddy like streams, and the spaces around stones demonstrate the significance of emptiness.

*"Tea is made with water
drawn from the Mind
Whose depth is beyond measure . . ."*

"The shadow of the
bamboo sweeps
the stair
All night long.
Yet not a mote of
dust is stirred.
The moonbeams
penetrate
To the bottom
of the pool,
Yet in the water not
a trace is left."

"The great path has no gates,
Thousands of roads enter it.
When one passes through
this gateless gate
He walks freely between
heaven and earth."

GLOSSARY

Age-joro: a courtesan.

Amaterasu: literally, "Great Divinity Illuminating Heaven"; the revered Shinto sun goddess from whom the Japanese imperial family claimed descent.

Ashigaru: literally, "light-foot"; peasant infantry troops originally armed with long spears but after the mid-to-late 16th century often armed with muskets.

Ashikaga: the military house whose shoguns ruled Japan in the name of the emperor for more than 200 years, from 1336 to 1573, during which time the country was almost constantly in a state of civil strife.

Bakufu: literally, "tent government"; originally, the field headquarters of a general during war; later, the name of the military government established by the shoguns, also known as the shogunate.

Buddhism: one of the major religions of China, the goal of which is to obtain spiritual perfection and thereby achieve nirvana; introduced into Japan in the mid-sixth century, and thereafter influencing and influenced by Shinto.

Buke Shohatto: literally, "Laws for Military Households"; laws first issued in 1615 that specified the obligation of the daimyo to the shogun and were the legal basis for control of the daimyo by the *bakufu.*

Bunraku: puppet theater developed in 17th-century Kyoto using puppets two or more feet tall manipulated by black-clad puppeteers, with a narrative tale told by an off-stage chanter, accompanied by a samisen; also known as *joruri.*

Bushido: literally, "the Way of the Warrior"; the samurai warrior's traditional code of loyalty, honor, bravery, self-discipline, and simple living.

Chado: the ritual for preparing, serving, and drinking tea; the ceremony includes tranquil reflection of, for example, a scroll painting, art object, or poem.

Cho: urban administrative districts, also called wards.

Concubine: a secondary wife, with lower social status and fewer rights than the primary wife.

Confucianism: a central Chinese philosophy based on the teachings of Confucius; originally imported into Japan around the sixth century and later used to buttress the authority of the Tokugawa shoguns.

Consort: the wife of an emperor, or any of an emperor's female companions, secondary wives, or concubines.

Courtesan: an exclusive, high-class prostitute, trained in music, conversation, and the arts; the so-cial graces; and the art of pleasing men. Clients were men of rank or wealth.

Courtier: an attendant at the court of the emperor.

Crown prince: the male heir apparent to the throne.

Curtain dais: a bedchamber consisting of a large wooden platform, about two feet high, with pillars at each corner holding a frame from which curtains hung, enclosing the platform.

Daimyo: originally, a large private landowner; by the late 15th century, powerful provincial barons who had total control over their territories, were subservient to no one, and were at war with each other. After the Tokugawa shogunate was established, the daimyo became vassals of the shogun, with their powers greatly reduced, and subject to the laws of the shogun in the Buke Shohatto.

Daoism: a mystical philosophy and religion based on searching for harmony with the Dao (the Way); one of the most important philosophies governing Chinese behavior and thought, imported into Japan in the seventh century and thereafter influencing Japanese culture.

Divination: the art or act of foretelling the future, revealing the will of the deities, and interpreting good and bad omens using various magical means.

Domaru: lightweight, wraparound iron body armor that fastened on the side or back, worn by samurai infantrymen; also called *haramaki.*

Emperor: the supreme ruler of Japan, considered to be a divine descendant of the sun goddess but who, for much of Japanese history, was only a figurehead, with the control of the country held by either a regent or a shogun.

Empress: the wife or consort of the emperor. In Japan, there could be empresses of several degrees, including grand empress and reigning empress.

Enlightenment: in Buddhism, a state of spiritual perfection in which one has achieved perfect wisdom, compassion, tranquillity, and a state of no desire and has recognized the essential oneness of all things.

Exorcism: to cast out evil spirits—considered to be the cause of illness—by incantation, command, prayer, or other rites.

Feudalism: in Japan, the system of relationships between the shogun and the daimyo, based upon the granting of fiefs by the shogun to the daimyo who, in return, pledged to the shogun their political and military support and allegiance. Similar pledges linked each daimyo to his own subordinates.

Fief: the land (and the peasants who lived on it) owned by the shogun but granted by him to a daimyo who then was free to hold and rule his fief, so long as he lived up to his oath of fealty to the shogun and obeyed the Buke Shohatto.

Floating world: name given to the colorful, exciting, sensual, and extravagant lifestyle of the Genroku era, during which literature, drama, and the arts flourished; also known as *ukiyo.*

Fudai: the daimyo who supported Tokugawa Ieyasu prior to the Battle of Sekigahara in 1600, which earned them (and their descendants) positions of trust in the shogunate; also called Hereditary Vassals.

Fujiwara: the enormously wealthy clan that, from the mid-ninth century to the mid-12th century, acted as regents to the emperors of Japan, monopolized court offices, and possessed nearly sovereign power.

Genji: another name for the Minamoto warrior family; also the name of the main fictional character in Murasaki Shikibu's masterpiece of the Heian period, *The Tale of Genji.*

Genroku era: the period from 1688 to 1704, when merchants prospered; Edo, Kyoto, and Osaka developed vibrant urban cultures; and puppet and live theater, poetry, prose, and the arts thrived.

Giri: literally, "duty"; obligation to one's family, class, society, or superior, generally depicted in Genroku-era puppet plays and domestic dramas as battling against *ninjo* (love or human emotions).

Go: a board game for two, played with 181 black and 180 white flat, round disks called stones on a square wooden board, the object being to conquer territory through strategic placement of the stones.

Grand empress: the wife of an ex-emperor.

Hachiman: the Shinto war god, one of the most popular of the Shinto deities and the patron god of all warriors.

Haikai: unorthodox or comic linked verses of 17 and 14 syllables composed by a group of poets. The first 17-syllable link later came to stand on its own and was called the haiku.

Haiku: a popular form of Japanese lyric poetry consisting of three unrhymed lines of 5, 7, and 5 syllables each, with the subject matter originally confined to nature but later expanded to include other subjects.

Hara-kiri: literally, "belly cutting"; a common term used for *seppuku* ("disembowelment"), the customary way in which samurai committed ritual suicide.

Hatamoto: literally "bannerman"; a direct retainer of the shogun generally appointed to an administrative position in the shogunate, with either an annual stipend or a small fief.

Heian era: the period from 794 to 1185, also known as the Peace and Tranquillity Era, when the Fujiwara clan dominated the political scene, the aristocracy accumulated great wealth, and the arts flourished.

Heike: another name for the Taira warrior family.

Hojo clan: an important military house that dominated the Kamakura shogunate by acting as regent for the shogun.

House: a merchant's enterprise, referring to both the business and the family that owned it; also used for military clans and their subordinates.

Hungry ghosts: in Buddhism, the name given to ancestors being punished for their excesses in life, whose karma is too good to permit them to be reborn as demons but not good enough to allow them to be reborn in higher states. They are thus condemned to roam the earth as hungry ghosts.

Iberians: inhabitants of the Iberian Peninsula, specifically, natives of Spain or Portugal.

Ise Shrine: the most sacred shrine in Shinto, dedicated to Amaterasu, the sun goddess, to which all Japanese tried to make a pilgrimage.

Jidaimono: history plays about love, honor, and revenge in noble samurai houses, developed during the Genroku era and performed as part of a longer kabuki program.

Joruri: the puppet theater, better known as bunraku.

Kabuki: A form of theater begun in the 17th century in Kyoto that originally featured songs and lively folk dances with rudimentary plots but that changed over the years to include historical and domestic dramas interspersed with dance plays and songs.

Kamakura bakufu: the military government established in Kamakura by the Minamoto clan at the end of the 12th century; it was quickly taken over and run by the Hojo clan as regents for the shoguns.

Kami: in Shinto, the vital forces of all things in nature and the native deities or spirits of Japan, including mythical figures or objects of nature as well as deified historical individuals.

Kamikaze: literally, "divine winds"; the typhoons of 1274 and 1281 that saved Japan from the Mongol invasions.

Kana: the Japanese phonetic, syllabic writing system.

Kannon: the Buddhist goddess of infinite compassion and mercy, one of the most popular of the Buddhist deities.

Kano school of artists: a school of ink painting that was Japanese in spirit but influenced by Chinese technique; characteristics include bold brush work and sharpness of outline.

Kare-san-sui: literally, "dry landscape"; a dry garden primarily featuring rocks, white pebbles, or sand (often raked into intricate patterns) and possibly one or more trees.

Karma: in Buddhism, the belief that one's actions, either good or bad, are always repaid with rewards or retribution in this life or in subsequent incarnations and that actions, therefore, affect the future course of one's existence.

Kicho: literally, "curtain of state"; a portable frame, generally about six feet high and of varying widths, curtained with an opaque material, used to protect females from view when receiving male visitors.

Kimono: a long, wide-sleeved robe, often elaborately decorated and usually belted with an obi, worn by both men and women as an outer garment, frequently in layers, one over another.

Koan: in Zen Buddhism, a paradoxical riddle or statement designed to free the mind and help achieve Enlightenment.

Kosode: literally, "small-sleeved garment"; a narrow-sleeved kimono, belted with an obi, worn by both men and women as an outer garment.

Koto: originally, any stringed instrument, but later, any of a variety of horizontal plucked instruments, the most common having a body made of paulownia wood and 13 strings and bridges.

Lacquer: a clear or colored coating, made from the sap of the lacquer tree, used to give a smooth, hard finish and a high gloss to the surface of an object and if applied in many layers, capable of being carved.

Land of the Rising Sun: another name for Japan.

Lunation: the time between two successive new moons, of 29 or 30 days in duration, on which the Japanese calendar system was based.

Matchlock musket: a shoulder gun carried by foot soldiers, used in Japan after the late 16th century, with a mechanical firing device to ignite the gunpowder.

Minamoto: one of two powerful late-11th-century warrior families, the Minamoto competed with the Taira family for control of the country; the family's leader established the military government known as the Kamakura *bakufu;* also called Genji.

Mise-joro: literally, "shown prostitutes"; common prostitutes who were displayed behind lattices to potential customers outside.

Mongol: any of a group of tribes from the steppes of central Asia that were united under Chinggis Khan; they conquered much of China and, under Khubilai Khan, attempted in the 13th century to conquer Japan.

Naginata: a weapon consisting of a long pole fitted with a one- to two-foot-long metal blade with a slightly curved end somewhat similar to the end of a scythe.

Next-morning letter: a letter sent the following morning (if all had gone well) by a suitor to the lady he was wooing after spending the night with her behind her curtain of state.

Ninjo: human emotions, such as kindness, passion, and love, generally depicted in Genroku-era puppet plays, drama, and novels in a battle against *giri* ("duty").

No: the classic, aristocratic, highly stylized drama of Japan, developed in the 14th century.

No-mind-ness: in Zen Buddhism, another term for Enlightenment.

Noren: a dark-blue cloth banner bearing a merchant's insignia, hung over the door of his establishment both to keep out heat and dust and to advertise his business.

Obi: a sash made of stiff silk worn by both men and women around the waist of a kosode or kimono.

Onnagata: female impersonators; in kabuki, men who acted women's roles.

Oyoroi: literally, "great harness"; in the Heian era, the boxlike suit of armor with a paneled skirt worn by warriors.

Phoenix: a large mythical bird of ancient legend, appearing in both Egyptian and Eastern myths; associated with sun worship and regarded as a symbol of fire or of death, resurrection, and immortality, often used as a decorative element in art.

Posting station: on the five state highways of Japan, government-run facilities that offered transportation and lodging at government-fixed rates.

Principal marriage: in polygamous marriages, usually, but not necessarily, the first marriage made, with its hierarchical distinction often not readily apparent to society but usually quite obvious within the privacy of the household.

Rango: a game in which women tried to balance as many go stones as they could on a single finger.

Ray: any of a number of different ocean fishes with a flattened, disklike body, a mouth on the underside of the body, large, winglike pectoral fins, and a long slender tail, frequently terminated with a sharp spine, capable of inflicting painful shocks or stings.

Reigning empress: the wife of the current emperor.

Ronin: literally, "wave men"; samurai who, after the reorganization of fiefs and the establishment of peace by the Tokugawa shogunate, were left unemployed, without a master or income.

Rosary: in Japanese Buddhism, a string of 112 wooden beads used as an aid in repeating mantras.

Saffron paste: a type of make-up used by women to paint a red dot on the center of the lips to make the mouth appear smaller.

Sake: a Japanese alcoholic beverage, often erroneously called a wine, made from fermented rice with a sweet, sherrylike flavor, considered to be the drink of the Shinto *kami.*

Samisen: a three-stringed Japanese musical

instrument resembling a banjo but with a very long neck.

Samurai: literally, "one who serves"; originally, a personal attendant to an overlord. Later, any of a class of expert professional warriors in the service of a daimyo or shogun, either mounted or on foot, armed with bows, two swords, and a dagger. Samurai adhered to the strict code of behavior known as bushido and were at the top of the Japanese class system; many became overlords themselves.

Satori: in Zen Buddhism, the moment of Enlightenment, usually attained through prolonged meditation, discipline, and concentration but also occurring abruptly and spontaneously.

Scroll: paper wound around a spindle and used for writing a document or painting a picture.

Scroll painting: in Japan, a painting done in ink on a roll of silk or paper, painted either as hanging scrolls, sized and designed to be hung on a wall, or hand scrolls, to be unrolled from right to left.

Secondary wife: any wife other than the primary wife, with lower social status and fewer rights than the primary wife.

Seii-taishogun: literally, "barbarian-suppressing commander in chief"; more commonly called shogun.

Sengoku Jidai: literally, "Age of the Country at War"; the period from the middle of the 15th century to the end of the 16th, when battles over shogunal succession kept Japan in a constant state of civil strife.

Seppuku: literally, "disembowelment"; the manner in which samurai traditionally committed ritual suicide; also called hara-kiri.

Sewamono: domestic plays written during the Genroku era, focusing on urban society, as opposed to court society.

Shinden: in Heian-period mansions, the central building that faced south onto an open court and to which subsidiary eastern and western buildings were attached by corridors.

Shinto: literally, "the Way of the Gods"; the native religion of Japan, an animistic system of beliefs developed from prehistoric practices characterized by a lack of formal doctrine and the belief that all things in nature have their own vital forces, spirits, or gods, called kami, that must be worshiped.

Shoen: from about the eighth century to the late 15th century, any of the private, tax-exempt estates held by high officials, the aristocracy, temples, shrines, clans, or warlords, many of which, over time, became enormous, independent from and immune to the civil authority of the state.

Shogun: originally, the title given to a number of military leaders commissioned to subdue rebellious natives in northern Japan but later, used to refer to the military dictator of Japan.

Shogunate: the government, rule, or office of a shogun; during those periods when the shogun exercised political control over Japan, synonymous with the term *bakufu.*

Sudden lords: name given by the aristocracy to newly rich warriors who sought to join the courtly life in Kyoto.

Sumo wrestling: Japanese wrestling, a highly ritualistic sport in which two men of immense size try to propel each other out of the 15-foot diameter ring or force any part of the opponent's body, other than the feet, to touch the floor.

Sushi: a Japanese staple consisting of vinegar-flavored rice cakes garnished with any number of other foods, such as raw or cooked fish, eggs, seaweed, or vegetables, served cold.

Sutra: in Buddhism, a scriptural narrative, especially one considered to be a writing, speech, or saying of the Buddha, or a collection of such materials.

Tachi: a long sword used by Heian and early-medieval Japanese warriors.

Taika: beginning in 645, a series of political reforms that strengthened the central government, extended the emperor's control over all of Japan, and imposed an orderly government administrative system on the state.

Taira: one of two powerful warrior clans that arose in the late 11th century, it competed with the Minamoto clan for control of Japan; also called Heike.

Tanto: short daggers carried by warriors into battle.

Tax rice: a tax payment in rice, made by peasants to their landlords. The rice was then converted by the landlord into gold and silver.

Third Night Rice Cakes: a ceremony that occurred two nights after the nuptials, when the bridegroom was "discovered" in the bride's bed by her mother, was given three rice cakes to eat, donned clothing provided by the bride's parents, and joined his new in-laws in a feast. Thereafter, the couple was considered married.

Three Houses and the Kinsmen: term given to members of the Tokugawa clan and its branches who lived in the mansions closest to the shogun's castle in Edo.

Tokaido: the highway from Edo to Kyoto, one of five government-built and controlled highways. The government offered security, food, and lodging along these routes at various checkpoints and posting stations.

Tokonoma: a ceremonial alcove in which a hanging scroll and flower arrangement or art object were placed.

Tokugawa: the warrior clan that descended from the Minamoto clan, completed the unification of Japan, and established the shogunate at Edo.

Tokugawa shogunate: name given to the military government that unified Japan and ruled the country from 1603 to 1868, a period noted for its peace and prosperity; also known as the Edo *bakufu.*

Tokyo: the modern name for Edo, renamed and made the official capital of Japan after the emperor's restoration to power in 1868.

Torii: the gateway into a Shinto shrine, which separates the secular world from the spiritual world. The gateway consists of two upright wooden pillars with two horizontal crossbeams and may be very plain or highly decorative.

Tozama: vassals who swore allegiance to Tokugawa Ieyasu only after he defeated them at the Battle of Sekigahara and so were never fully trusted; also called Outside Lords.

Typhoon: a tropical cyclone in the western Pacific or Indian Oceans with exceedingly high winds.

Ukiyo: literally, "the floating world"; the name given to the colorful, exciting, sensual, and extravagant lifestyle of the Genroku era during which the arts, literature, and drama flourished.

Ukiyo-zoshi: literally, "books of the floating world"; the name given to the popular novels depicting the lives of the 17th-century bourgeoisie.

Waka: the classic Japanese poetic form, severely elegant in style, typically consisting of only 31 syllables.

Wakashu: in kabuki, the name given to the young men who took over the roles of the actresses when women were banned from the stage. Many of the *wakashu* were also prostitutes and were eventually also banned from acting.

Warlord: a military commander who might or might not give allegiance to an overlord or national government but who exerted full dictatorial power within his own territory.

Wedded rocks: in Ise Bay off Japan's southern coast, two rocks that serve as a sacred gateway to a Shinto shrine. A straw rope, used to mark a sacred place, joins the rocks and a symbolic torii stands atop the "husband" rock.

Woodblock printing method: the earliest known relief printing method, invented in ninth-century China, utilizing an engraving of text and/or pictures carved on a block of wood to create a design subsequently printed on paper.

Zen: a school of Buddhist thought, imported from China, that holds that Enlightenment is available to anyone but can be achieved only by sudden revelation following meditation.

PRONUNCIATION GUIDE

Adachi Yasumori (ah-dah-chee yah-soo-moh-ree)
Age-joro (ah-geh-joh-roh)
Asai Ryoi (ah-sye ryoh-ee)
Ashigaru (ah-shee-gah-roo)
Ashikaga Takauji (ah-shee-kah-gah tah-kah-oo-jee)
Ashikaga Yoshiaki (ah-shee-kah-gah yoh-shee-ah-kee)
Atsuhira (ah-tsoo-hee-rah)
Atsuyasu (ah-tsoo-yah-soo)
Bakufu (bah-koo-foo)
Buke Shohatto (boo-keh shoh-haht-toh)
Bunraku (boon-rah-koo)
Bushido (boo-shee-doh)
Chihaya (chee-hah-yah)
Chikamatsu Monzaemon (chee-kah-mah-tsoo mohn-zah-eh-mohn)
Chushingura (choo-sheen-goo-rah)
Daimyo (dye-myoh)
Echigoya (eh-chee-goh-yah)
Edo (eh-doh)
Fudai (foo-dye)
Fujiwara Michinaga (foo-jee-whah-rah mee-chee-nah-gah)
Funanoe (foo-nah-noh-eh)
Genji (gehn-jee)
Genroku (gehn-roh-koo)
Giri (ghee-ree)
Go-Daigo (goh-dye-goh)
Go-Ichijo (goh-ee-chee-joe)
I Iachirobei (hah-chee-roh-bay)
Haikai (hye-kye)
Haiku (hye-koo)
Hara-kiri (hah-rah-kee-ree)
Heian (hay-ahn)
Heike (hay-keh)
Hidetsugu (hee-deh-tsoo-goo)
Hideyori (hee-deh-yoh-ree)
I Iiei (hee-ay)
Himeji (hee-meh-jee)
Hokkaido (hohk-kye-doh)
Hon'ami Koetsu (hohn-ah-mee koh-eh-tsoo)
Horikawa (hoh-ree-kah-wah)

Hyogo (hyoh-goh)
Ichijo (ee-chee-joh)
Ihara Saikaku (ee-hah-rah sye-kah-koo)
Imagawa Yoshimoto (ee-mah-gah-wah yoh-shee-moh-toh)
Ise (ee-seh)
Jidaimono (jee-dye-moh-noh)
Joruri (joh-roo-ree)
Kaneie (kah-neh-ee-eh)
Kare-san-sui (kah-reh-sahn-soo-ee)
Kasagi (kah-sah-ghee)
Kicho (kee-choh)
Kinai (kee-nye)
Koan (koh-ahn)
Korechika (koh-reh-chee-kah)
Kosode (koh-soh-deh)
Kusunoki Masashige (koo-soo-noh-kee mah-sah-shee-geh)
Masamune (mah-sah-moo-neh)
Masasue (mah-sah-soo-eh)
Masatsura (mah-sah-tsoo-rah)
Matsujiro (mah-tsoo-jee-roh)
Matsuo Basho (mah-tsoo-oh bah-shoh)
Mikawa (mee-kah-wah)
Mise-joro (mee-seh-joh-roh)
Murasaki Shikibu (moo-rah-sah-kee shee-kee-boo)
Nagahide (nah-gah-hee-deh)
Naginata (nah-ghee-nah-tah)
Nihon Shoki (nee-hohn shoh-kee)
Nijo (nee-joh)
Ninigi (nee-nee-ghee)
Nitta Yoshisada (neet-tah yoh-shee-sah-dah)
Oichi (oh-ee-chee)
Oyoroi (oh-yoh-roh-ee)
Rango (rahn-goh)
Ronin (roh-neen)
Saiko (sye-koh)
Samisen (sah-mee-sehn)
Samurai (sah-moo-rye)
Sei Shonagon (say shoh-nah-gohn)
Seii-taishogun (say-ee-tye-shoh-goon)
Seikenji (say-kehn-jee)

Sekigahara (seh-kee-gah-hah-rah)
Sengoku Jidai (sehn-goh-koo jee-dye)
Sen no Rikyu (sehn noh ree-kyoo)
Seppuku (sehp-poo-koo)
Sewamono (seh-wah-moh-noh)
Shikoku (shee-koh-koo)
Shimabara (shee-mah-bah-rah)
Shinmachi (sheen-mah-chee)
Shoshi (shoh-shee)
Sonezaki-Shinchi (soh-neh-zah-kee-sheen-chee)
Sotoba Komachi (soh-toh-bah koh-mah-chee)
Suruga (soo-roo-gah)
Tachi (tah-chee)
Tadayoshi (tah-dah-yoh-shee)
Taika (tye-kah)
Taira Kiyomori (tye-rah kee-yoh-moh-ree)
Takahide (tah-kah-hee-deh)
Takeda Katsuyori (tah-keh-dah kah-tsoo-yoh-ree)
Takeshiuchi Sukune (tah-keh-shee-oo-chee soo-koo-neh)
Takezaki Suenaga (tah-keh-zah-kee soo-eh-nah-gah)
Tanegashima (tah-neh-gah-shee-mah)
Teishi (tay-shee)
Tendai (tehn-dye)
Tenka fubu (tehn-kah foo-boo)
Tokaido (toh-kye-doh)
Tokubei (toh-koo-bay)
Tokugawa Ieyasu (toh-koo-gah-wah ee-eh-yah-soo)
Tomoe Gozen (toh-moh-eh goh-zehn)
Torii (toh-ree-ee)
Toyotomi Hideyoshi (toh-yoh-toh-mee hee-deh-yoh-shee)
Tsuchimikado (tsoo-chee-mee-kah-doh)
Tsunayoshi (tsoo-nah-yoh-shee)
Tsurehide (tsoo-reh-hee-deh)
Tsushima (tsoo-shee-mah)
Ukiyo (oo-kee-yoh)
Yorimichi (yoh-ree-mee-chee)
Yoshitsune (yoh-shee-tsoo-neh)
Zeami (zeh-ah-mee)

ACKNOWLEDGMENTS AND PICTURE CREDITS

ACKNOWLEDGMENTS

The editors wish to thank the following individuals and institutions for their valuable assistance in the preparation of this volume:
T. Egami, Golden Pavilion Temple, Kyoto; Staff of Fujita Museum of Art, Osaka; Staff of Tourism Office of Futami Town, Futami, Mie Prefecture; Staff of Historiographical Institute, the University of Tokyo, Tokyo; O. Hizume, Otsu City Museum of History, Otsu; M. Igaki, Suntory Museum of Art, Tokyo; Greg Irvine, Victoria and Albert Museum, London; Jimyoin temple, Nara Prefecture; Jingoji temple, Kyoto; Heidrun Klein, Bildarchiv Preussischer Kulturbesitz, Berlin; K. Kuniteru, Kawagoe City Museum, Kawagoe; S. Matsubara, Tokyo National Museum, Tokyo; T. Matsumoto, Nijo Castle, Kyoto; R. Morimoto, Japan Weather Association, Tokyo; T. Nagai, Mitsui Research Institute for Social and Economic History, Tokyo; H. Nakamura, Osaka Castle Museum, Osaka; Nanzenji temple, Kyoto; Takehiko Noguchi; Y. Saeki, Hofu Tenmangu shrine, Hofu, Yamaguchi Prefecture; S. Sakaguchi, Kyoto National Museum, Kyoto; H. Sato, Yamagata Museum of Art, Yamagata; Stephan von der Schulenburg, Museum für Kunsthandwerk, Frankfurt am Main; S. Shirono, Yamato Bunkakan Museum, Nara; K. Suzuki, Kawagoe City Museum, Kawagoe; J. Yuzurihara, Okura Cultural Foundation, Tokyo.

BIBLIOGRAPHY

BOOKS

Addiss, Stephen. *Zenga and Nanga*. New Orleans: New Orleans Museum of Art, 1976.

Arai Hakuseki:
The Armour Book in Honcho-Gunkiko. Trans. by Y. Otsuka, ed. by H. Russell Robinson. Rutland, Vt.: Charles E. Tuttle, 1964.
The Sword Book in Honcho Gunkiko and the Book of Samé Ko Hi Sei Gi of Inaba Tsurio. Rutland, Vt.: Charles E. Tuttle, 1963.

Arms and Armor of the Samurai. New York: Crescent Books, 1996.

Asian Art Museum of San Francisco. *The Art of Japan*. San Francisco: Chronicle Books, 1991.

Bayrd, Edwin. *Kyoto*. New York: Newsweek, 1974.

Beard, Mary R. *The Force of Women in Japanese History*. Washington, D.C.: Public Affairs Press, 1953.

Berry, Mary Elizabeth. *Hideyoshi*. Cambridge, Mass.: Harvard University Press, 1989.

The Cambridge History of Japan, Vol. 1: Ancient Japan. Ed. by Delmer M. Brown. Cambridge: Cambridge University Press, 1993.

The Cambridge History of Japan, Vol. 3: Medieval Japan. Ed. by Kozo Yamamura. Cambridge: Cambridge University Press, 1990.

The Cambridge History of Japan, Vol. 4: Early Modern Japan. Ed. by John Whitney Hall. Cambridge: Cambridge University Press, 1991.

Clark, Timothy. *Ukiyo-e Paintings in the British Museum*. Washington, D.C.: Smithsonian Institution Press, 1992.

Collcutt, Martin, Marius Jansen, and Isao Kumakura. *The Cultural Atlas of the World: Japan*. Alexandria, Va.: Stonehenge Press, 1988.

Cook, Harry. *Samurai*. New York: Sterling, 1993.

Cooper, Michael, ed. *They Came to Japan: An Anthology of European Reports on Japan, 1543-1640*. Berkeley: University of California Press, 1965.

Corr, William. *Adams the Pilot: The Life and Times of Captain William Adams, 1564-1620*. Folkestone, Kent, England: Japan Library, 1995.

Court and Bakufu in Japan: Essays in Kamakura History. Ed. by Jeffrey P. Mass. New Haven, Conn.: Yale University Press, 1982.

Craig, Albert M., and Donald H. Shively, eds. *Personality in Japanese History*. Berkeley: University of California Press, 1970.

Cunningham, Michael R. *The Triumph of Japanese Style: 16th-Century Art in Japan*. Cleveland: Cleveland Museum of Art, 1991.

Dalbt, Liza Crihfield. *Kimono: Fashioning Culture*. New Haven, Conn.: Yale University Press, 1993.

Dunn, C. J. *Everyday Life in Traditional Japan*. Tokyo: Charles E. Tuttle, 1969.

Early Masters: Ukiyo-e Prints and Paintings, from 1660 to 1750. New York: Japan Society Gallery, 1991.

Edo and Paris: Urban Life and the State in the Early Modern Era. Ed. by James L. McClain, John M. Merriman, and Ugawa Kaoru. Ithaca, N.Y.: Cornell University Press, 1994.

Elisseeff, Danielle, and Vadime Elisseeff. *Art of Japan*. Trans. by I. Mark Paris. New York: Harry N. Abrams, 1985.

Feminine Image: Women of Japan. Honolulu: Honolulu Academy of Arts, 1985.

Fréderic, Louis. *Daily Life in Japan at the Time of the Samurai, 1185-1603*. Trans. by Eileen M. Lowe. New York: Praeger, 1972.

Freer Gallery of Art, comp. *Freer Gallery of Art, Vol. 2: Japan*. Tokyo: Kodansha, [1971].

Friday, Karl F. *Hired Swords: The Rise of Private Warrior Power in Early Japan*. Stanford, Calif.: Stanford University Press, 1992.

Fury of the Northmen: TimeFrame AD 800-1000 (Time Frame series). Alexandria, Va.: Time-Life Books, 1988.

Great Historical Figures of Japan. Tokyo: Japan Culture Institute, 1978.

Grossberg, Kenneth Alan. *Japan's Renaissance: The Politics of the Muromachi Bakufu*. Cambridge, Mass.: Harvard University Press, 1981.

Guth, Christine. *Art of Edo Japan: The Artist and the City, 1615-1868*. New York: Harry N. Abrams, 1996.

Haberland, Detlef. *Engelbert Kaempfer, 1651-1716*. Trans. by Peter Hogg. London: British Library, 1996.

Hall, John Whitney. *Japan: From Prehistory to Modern Times*. New York: Delacorte Press, 1970.

Hall, John W., and Marius B. Jansen, eds. *Studies in the Institutional History of Early Modern Japan*. Princeton, N.J.: Princeton University Press, 1968.

Hall, John Whitney, Nagahara Keiji, and Kozo Yamamura, eds. *Japan before Tokugawa*. Princeton, N.J.: Princeton University Press, 1981.

Hempel, Rose. *The Golden Age of Japan, 794-1192*. Trans. by Katherine Watson. New York: Rizzoli, 1983.

The Heritage of Japanese Art. Tokyo: Kodansha International, 1981.

Hideyoshi, Toyotomi. *101 Letters of Hideyoshi*. Trans. and ed. by Adriana Boscaro. Tokyo: Sofia University, 1975.

Hirschmeier, Johannes, and Tsunehiko Yui. *The Development of Japanese Business, 1600-1980*. London: George Allen & Unwin, 1981.

Hisamatsu, Sen'ichi. *Biographical Dictionary of Japanese Literature*. Tokyo: Kodansha International, 1976.

House of Mitsui, A Record of Three Centuries: Past History and Present Enterprises. Tokyo: Mitsui Gomei Kaisha, 1933.

Inoura, Yoshinobu, and Toshio Kawatake. *The Traditional Theater of Japan*. Tokyo: Japan Foundation, 1981.

Ito, Teiji. *The Gardens of Japan*. Tokyo: Kodansha International, 1984.

Japan: The Shaping of Daimyo Culture, 1185-1868. Washington, D.C.: National Gallery of Art, 1988.

Kageyama, Haruki. *The Arts of Shinto*. Trans. by Christine Guth. New York: Weatherhill, 1973.

Katsuhiko, Mizuno. *Masterpieces of Japanese Garden Art: Western Kyoto*. Trans. by Gretchen Mittwer. Kyoto: Kyoto Shoin, 1992.

Keane, Marc P. *Japanese Garden Design*. Rutland, Vt.: Charles E. Tuttle, 1996.

Keene, Donald:
No: The Classical Theatre of Japan. Tokyo: Kodansha International, 1966.
Travelers of a Hundred Ages. New York: Henry Holt, 1989.
World within Walls: Japanese Literature of the Pre-Modern Era, 1600-1867. New York: Holt, Rinehart and Winston, 1976.

Keene, Donald, trans. *Four Major Plays of Chikamatsu*. New York: Columbia University Press, 1961.

Kennedy, Alan. *Japanese Costume: History and Tradition*. Paris: Editions Adam Biro, 1990.

Kidder, J. Edward, Jr. *The Art of Japan*. New York: Park Lane, 1985.

Kinosita, Yetaro. *The Past and Present of Japanese Commerce*. New York: AMS Press, 1968.

Kirkwood, Kenneth P. *Renaissance in Japan*. Rutland, Vt.: Charles E. Tuttle, 1970.

Kokusai Bunka Shinkokai (Society for International Cultural Relations), eds. *Introduction to Classical Japanese Literature*. Westport, Conn.: Greenwood Press, 1970.

Kondo Ichitaro. *Japanese Genre Painting*. Trans. by Roy Andrew Miller. Rutland, Vt.: Charles E. Tuttle, 1961.

Lee, Sherman E. *Reflections of Reality in Japanese Art*. Cleveland: Cleveland Museum of Art, 1983.

Lehmann, Jean-Pierre. *The Roots of Modern Japan*. New York: St. Martin's Press, 1982.

Leonard, Jonathan Norton, and the Editors of Time-Life Books. *Early Japan* (Great Ages of Man series). New York: Time-Life Books, 1968.

Lu, David J. *Japan*. Armonk, N.Y.: East Gate, 1997.

McAlpine, Helen, and William McAlpine. *Japanese Tales and Legends*. Oxford: Oxford University Press, 1958.

McCullough, Helen Craig, trans.:
Okagami, the Great Mirror: Fujiwara Michinaga (966-1027) and His Times. Princeton, N.J.: Princeton University Press, 1980.

The Taiheiki: A Chronicle of Medieval Japan. Rutland, Vt.: Charles E. Tuttle, 1959.

The Tale of the Heike. Stanford, Calif.: Stanford University Press, 1988.

McCullough, William H., and Helen Craig McCullough, trans. *The Tale of Flowering Fortunes: Annals of Japanese Aristocratic Life in the Heian Period, Vol. 1.* Stanford, Calif.: Stanford University Press, 1980.

The Mongol Conquests: TimeFrame AD 1200-1300 (Time Frame series). Alexandria, Va.: Time-Life Books, 1989.

Morris, Ivan:
The Nobility of Failure. New York: Holt, Rinehart and Winston, 1962.
The World of the Shining Prince: Court Life in Ancient Japan. New York: Alfred A. Knopf, 1964.

Morris, Ivan, ed. *The Tale of Genji Scroll.* Tokyo: Kodansha International, 1971.

Murasaki Shikibu:
Murasaki Shikibu: Her Diary and Poetic Memoirs. Trans. by Richard Bowring. Princeton, N.J.: Princeton University Press, 1982.
The Tale of Genji. New York: Alfred A. Knopf, 1991.

Murphy, Wendy B., and the Editors of Time-Life Books. *Japanese Gardens* (Encyclopedia of Gardening series). Alexandria, Va.: Time-Life Books, 1979.

Najita, Tetsuo. *Visions of Virtue in Tokugawa Japan.* Chicago: University of Chicago Press, 1987.

Nishiyama, Matsunosuke. *Edo Culture: Daily Life and Diversions in Urban Japan, 1600-1868.* Trans. and ed. by Gerald Groemer. Honolulu: University of Hawai`i Press, 1997.

Okudaira, Hideo. *Narrative Picture Scrolls.* Trans. by Elizabeth ten Grotenhuis. New York: Weatherhill, 1973.

Perrin, Noel. *Giving up the Gun: Japan's Reversion to the Sword, 1543-1879.* Boulder, Colo.: Shambhala, 1980.

Powers of the Crown: TimeFrame AD 1600-1700 (Time Frame series). Alexandria, Va.: Time-Life Books, 1989.

Roberson, John R. *Japan: From Shogun to Sony, 1543-1984.* New York: Atheneum, 1985.

Ross, Nancy Wilson. *Three Ways of Asian Wisdom: Hinduism, Buddhism, Zen and Their Significance for the West.* New York: Simon and Schuster, 1966.

Ross, Nancy Wilson, comp. and ed. *The World of Zen: An East-West Anthology.* New York: Vintage Books, 1960.

Saikaku, Ihara:
The Japanese Family Storehouse. Trans. by G. W. Sargent. Cambridge: Cambridge University Press, 1959.

The Life of an Amorous Woman: And Other Writings. Trans. and ed. by Ivan Morris. New York: New Directions Books, 1963.

Tales of Samurai Honor. Trans. by Caryl Ann Callahan. Tokyo: Monumenta Nipponica, 1981.

Sansom, George B.:
A History of Japan, To 1334. Stanford, Calif.: Stanford University Press, 1958.
A History of Japan, 1334-1615. Stanford, Calif.: Stanford University Press, 1961.
A History of Japan, 1615-1867. Stanford, Calif.: Stanford University Press, 1963.

Sato, Hiroaki. *Legends of the Samurai.* Woodstock, N.Y.: Overlook Press, 1995.

Schirokauer, Conrad. *A Brief History of Japanese Civilization.* Fort Worth, Tex.: Harcourt Brace, 1993.

Seattle Art Museum. *A Thousand Cranes.* San Francisco: Chronicle Books, 1987.

Sei Shonagon. *The Pillow Book of Sei Shonagon.* Trans. and ed. by Ivan Morris. New York: Columbia University Press, 1991.

Seigle, Cecilia Segawa. *Yoshiwara: The Glittering World of the Japanese Courtesan.* Honolulu: University of Hawaii Press, 1993.

Sen, Soshitsu. *Tea Life, Tea Mind.* Trans. and ed. by the Urasenke Foundation. New York: Weatherhill, 1979.

Shinoda, Minoru. *The Founding of the Kamakura Shogunate, 1180-1185.* New York: Columbia University Press, 1960.

Sichel, Marion. *Japan.* New York: Chelsea House, 1987.

Singer, Robert T. *Edo: Art in Japan, 1615-1868.* Washington, D.C.: National Gallery of Art, 1998.

Smith, Bradley. *Japan: A History in Art.* New York: Simon and Schuster, 1964.

Smith, Lawrence, Victor Harris, and Timothy Clark. *Japanese Art: Masterpieces in the British Museum.* London: British Museum, 1990.

Stanley-Baker, Joan. *Japanese Art.* London: Thames and Hudson, 1984.

Stevens, John. *Zenga: Brushstrokes of Enlightenment.* New Orleans: New Orleans Museum of Art, 1990.

Storry, Richard. *The Way of the Samurai.* London: Orbis, 1978.

Suzuki, Daisetz T. *Zen and Japanese Culture.* Princeton, N.J.: Princeton University Press, 1959.

Tames, Richard. *Servant of the Shogun.* New York: St. Martin's Press, 1987.

Tanaka, Sen'o. *The Tea Ceremony.* Tokyo: Kodansha International, 1973.

The Tokugawa Collection: The Japan of the Shoguns. Montreal: Montreal Museum of Fine Arts, 1989.

Totman, Conrad D.:
Early Modern Japan. Berkeley: University of

California Press, 1993.
Japan before Perry: A Short History. Berkeley: University of California Press, 1981.
Politics in the Tokugawa Bakufu. Cambridge, Mass.: Harvard University Press, 1967.

Tsunoda, Ryusaku, Wm. Theodore de Bary, and Donald Keene, comps. *Sources of Japanese Tradition.* New York: Columbia University Press, 1958.

Turnbull, Stephen:
Samurai. London: Arms and Armour Press, 1996.
Samurai Warfare. London: Arms and Armour Press, 1996.

Twelve Centuries of Japanese Art from the Imperial Collections. Washington, D.C.: Freer Gallery of Art, 1997.

Varley, H. Paul:
Imperial Restoration in Medieval Japan. New York: Columbia University Press, 1971.
Japanese Culture. Honolulu: University of Hawaii Press, 1984.
Japanese Culture: A Short History. New York: Praeger, 1973.
Samurai. New York: Delacorte Press, 1970.

Warlords, Artists, & Commoners: Japan in the Sixteenth Century. Ed. by George Elison and Bardwell L. Smith. Honolulu: University Press of Hawaii, 1981.

Warrior Rule in Japan. Ed. by Marius B. Jansen. Cambridge: Cambridge University Press, 1995.

Watts, Alan W. *The Way of Zen.* New York: Vintage Books, 1985.

Webb, Herschel. *The Japanese Imperial Institution in the Tokugawa Period.* New York: Columbia University Press, 1968.

Wiencek, Henry. *The Lords of Japan.* Chicago: Stonehenge Press, 1982.

Wright, Tom, and Mizuno Katsuhiko. *Zen Gardens.* Kyoto: Suiko Books, 1990.

Yoshikawa, Eiji. *The Heike Story.* Trans. by Fuki Wooyenaka Uramatsu. Rutland, Vt.: Charles E. Tuttle, 1956.

Zen Flesh, Zen Bones: A Collection of Zen & Pre-Zen Writings. Comp. by Paul Reps. Garden City, N.Y.: Anchor Books, 1989.

PERIODICALS

Harvard Journal of Asiatic Studies, Vol. 25, 1964-1965.
Harvard Journal of Asiatic Studies, Vol. 27, 1967.

OTHER SOURCES

Arts Council of Great Britain. *The Harari Collection of Japanese Paintings and Drawings.* Exhibition catalog. Victoria and Albert Museum, Jan. 14-Feb. 22, 1970.

The Shogun Age Exhibition. Tokyo: Shogun Age Exhibition Executive Committee, 1983.

INDEX

Page numbers in italics refer to illustrations or illustrated text.

Time-Life Books is a division of Time Life Inc.

TIME LIFE INC.
PRESIDENT and CEO: George Artandi

TIME-LIFE BOOKS
PUBLISHER/MANAGING EDITOR: Neil Kagan
VICE PRESIDENT, MARKETING: Joseph A. Kuna
VICE PRESIDENT, NEW PRODUCT
DEVELOPMENT: Amy Golden

What Life Was Like ®
AMONG SAMURAI AND SHOGUNS

EDITOR: Denise Dersin
DIRECTOR, NEW PRODUCT DEVELOPMENT:
Elizabeth D. Ward
DIRECTOR OF MARKETING:
Pamela R. Farrell

Deputy Editor: Marion Ferguson Briggs
Art Director: Alan Pitts
Text Editor: Jarelle S. Stein
Associate Editor/Research and Writing:
Sharon Kurtz Thompson
Senior Copyeditor: Mary Beth Oelkers-Keegan
Technical Art Specialist: John Drummond
Photo Coordinator: David Herod
Editorial Assistant: Christine Higgins

Special Contributors: Charlotte Anker, Ronald H. Bailey,
Ellen Phillips (chapter text); Gaye Brown, Christine
Hauser, Donna M. Lucey, Jane Martin, Marilyn Murphy
Terrell, Elizabeth Thompson (research-writing); Arlene
Borden, K. Ginger Crockett, Holly Downen, Ronald
K. Frank, Beth Levin (research); Janet Cave (editing);
Lina Baber Burton (glossary); Barbara L. Klein (index
and overread).

Correspondents: Christine Hinze (London), Christina
Lieberman (New York), Maria Vincenza Aloisi (Paris).
Valuable assistance was also provided by Angelika
Lemmer (Bonn), Midori Kai, Hiroko Tashiro, Tamae
Yoshida (Tokyo).

Director of Finance: Christopher Hearing
Directors of Book Production: Marjann Caldwell,
Patricia Pascale
Director of Publishing Technology: Betsi McGrath
Director of Photography and Research: John Conrad Weiser
Director of Editorial Administration: Barbara Levitt
Manager, Technical Services: Anne Topp
Senior Production Manager: Ken Sabol
Production Manager: Virginia Reardon
Quality Assurance Manager: James King
Chief Librarian: Louise D. Forstall

Consultant:
H. Mack Horton is a specialist in classical Japanese literature
and culture. An associate professor at the University of California at Berkeley, Dr. Horton is the author of *Song in an
Age of Discord,* a study of the linked-verse poet Socho and
literary life in the height of Japan's war-torn medieval era,
as well as a translation and commentary of the *Journal of
Socho,* which won the Japan-U.S. Friendship Commission
Prize for the translation of Japanese literature. Dr. Horton
has also written extensively on medieval poetic practice,
patronage, and canon formation, and on Japanese traditional
architecture. He is a contributor to the *Macmillan Dictionary
of Art,* the *Dictionary of Literary Biography,* the *Encyclopedia of
Japan,* and the *Haibungaku daijiten* (a dictionary of haikai literature). He is currently at work on a study and translation
of the earliest anthology of Japanese poetry, *Man'yoshu.*

First printing. Printed in U.S.A.
School and library distribution by Time-Life Education,
P.O. Box 85026, Richmond, Virginia 23285-5026.

TIME-LIFE is a trademark of Time Warner Inc. U.S.A.

Library of Congress Cataloging-in-Publication Data
What life was like among Samurai and Shoguns : Japan,
AD 1000-1700 / by the editors of Time-Life Books.
        p.   cm. —   (What life was like ; 13)
    Includes bibliographical references and index.
    ISBN 0-7835-5462-1
    1. Japan—Court and courtiers. 2. Rites and
ceremonies—Japan. 3. Japan—Civilization—To 1868.
I. Time-Life Books.   II. Series: What life was like
series ; 13.
DS824.W43 1999   99-10919
952—dc21   CIP

This volume is one in a series on world history that
uses contemporary art, artifacts, and personal accounts to
create an intimate portrait of daily life in the past.

Other volumes included in the *What Life Was Like* series:

Other Publications:
HISTORY
Our American Century
World War II
The American Story
Voices of the Civil War
The American Indians
Lost Civilizations
Mysteries of the Unknown
Time Frame
The Civil War
Cultural Atlas

COOKING
Weight Watchers® Smart Choice Recipe Collection
Great Taste~Low Fat
Williams-Sonoma Kitchen Library

SCIENCE/NATURE
Voyage Through the Universe

DO IT YOURSELF
Total Golf
How to Fix It
The Time-Life Complete Gardener
Home Repair and Improvement
The Art of Woodworking

TIME-LIFE KIDS
Student Library
Library of First Questions and Answers
A Child's First Library of Learning
I Love Math
Nature Company Discoveries
Understanding Science & Nature

For information on and a full description of any of
the Time-Life Books series listed above, please call
1-800-621-7026 or write:

Reader Information
Time-Life Customer Service
P.O. Box C-32068
Richmond, Virginia 23261-2068